A faith that endures

Meditations on Hebrews 11

Brian Croft

DayOne

Endorsements

I rejoice in Brian Croft's book because he reminds us from Hebrews 11 and 12 that Old Testament saints, and Jesus supremely, trusted in God. They persevered in faith even when their circumstances seemed to scream out that God's Word was untrue. Pastor Croft gives feet and hands to faith, showing us what it looks like in everyday life. May we follow those who have gone before us in faith, so that we, like them, will win an eternal reward.

Thomas R. Schreiner, James Buchanan Harrison Professor of New Testament Interpretation, The Southern Baptist Theological Seminary, Louisville, KY, USA

Brian Croft is a faithful shepherd of souls and an expositional preacher. These sermons, arising from that crucial context, will be valuable to other pastors and other believers in general who are hazarding their way to the Celestial City. Endurance is a theme often lacking in church discussion today but it is one of immense pastoral importance. Croft's book provides a timely, helpful, Christ-centered discussion of this important topic.

Ray Van Neste, Associate Professor of Biblical Studies, and Director, R. C. Ryan Center for Biblical Studies, Union University, Jackson, TN, USA
www.rayvanneste.com

It is not easy to hold fast. We see many faint and fall around us, and perhaps we wonder if we shall stand to the end. In this short and sweet treatment of Hebrews 11, Brian Croft encourages us to cling to God in Christ and so stand fast. Writing with sober yet joyful realism and with pastoral insight and earnestness, he defines the enduring faith of true believers before guiding us through the gallery of the faithful that the writer to the Hebrews has arrayed, pointing out for us that very faith in the lives of those who have gone before us, bringing us finally to the awe-inspiring, beautiful portrait of our Lord Christ. With plain and well-grounded exhortations, and with some particularly straight talking to Christ's under-shepherds, Brian calls us to cultivate the same precious, enduring faith, showing us why we should and how we may so run as to last the course.

Jeremy Walker, Pastor, Maidenbower Baptist Church, Crawley, UK, and co-author of A Portrait of Paul (Reformation Heritage Books)

Taking the examples of men and women of God from Hebrews 11, as well as those who have modeled enduring faith in his own life and experience, Pastor Brian Croft gives practical, pastoral, biblical, and Christ-centered counsel to aid believers in persevering in the way. I highly recommend this resource to pastors and laypeople alike.

Jim Savastio, Senior Pastor, The Reformed Baptist Church of Louisville, KY, USA

© Day One Publications 2011
First Edition 2011

Unless otherwise indicated, Scripture quotations taken from the New American Standard
Bible®, Copyright © 1960, 1962, 1963, 1968, 1971, 1972, 1973, 1975, 1977, 1995 by The
Lockman Foundation Used by permission. (www.Lockman.org)

British Library Cataloguing in Publication Data available

ISBN 978-1-84625-292-1

Published by Day One Publications
Ryelands Road, Leominster, HR6 8NZ

☎ 01568 613 740
FAX: 01568 611 473
email—sales@dayone.co.uk
web site—www.dayone.co.uk

Designed by Wayne McMaster and printed by Orchard Press, Cheltenham Ltd.

To the many faithful elderly saints of
Auburndale Baptist Church, Louisville,
Kentucky, who increased my faith through
their endurance in Christ firm until the end.

Acknowledgments

Special thanks to:

Joseph Gould, without whose tireless labor this book would not exist. He took my scattered, rough sermon transcripts and crafted them into a more coherent, flowing document from which to work. My deepest thanks go to him for his service to me in this regard.

Those who read and gave helpful feedback on this manuscript—in particular, Jason Adkins and Sarah Bowen, who went above and beyond in their service and efforts to make this book better. Thank you for your friendship and help throughout this project.

Scott Wells, Adam Embry, Adam Grusy, and Jason Adkins, my fellow laborers and co-pastors at Auburndale Baptist Church, for whom I am so grateful in connection with the message of this book. God uses them daily to encourage and strengthen me in the shepherding task we share together, so that we all might finish well.

Tom Schreiner, for your Foreword and your friendship.

My wife and children: you continue to be God's greatest gift to me in this life. Your love and care for me act as a tremendous motivation to endure faithfully.

The Chief Shepherd, Jesus Christ, who by his person and work saves me, keeps me, intercedes for me, and promises to sustain my faith, so that I may hold fast and endure until the end.

Contents

Foreword

The book of Hebrews contains the strongest warning passages in the New Testament, admonishing its readers to continue to persevere and threatening them with judgment if they fall away. For some, the warnings in Hebrews seem almost legalistic. The author of Hebrews throws down thunderbolts which terrify readers with the danger of apostasy. However, if the warnings in Hebrews seem to be out of character with the rest of the New Testament, we are either reading Hebrews wrongly or we are off-kilter in our reading of the rest of the New Testament; perhaps both are true. We may fail to see the urgent admonitions and warnings that permeate the rest of the New Testament. At the same time, we may misunderstand the nature of the warnings in Hebrews.

It is this last observation that I want to elaborate on here. The Hebrews were tempted to commit apostasy, but what was the false way which appealed to them? Apparently they desired to return to Old Testament religion. Perhaps they began to believe that the visible and repeated ritual of the sacrificial system would truly cleanse their consciences of sins. In any case, there is no indication that the Hebrews were tempted to stray from Christ because they wanted to live licentious lifestyles. They were not drawn to a life of sexual sin and wild parties. Instead, they were attracted by life under the old covenant and the Old Testament law. They had begun to think that the old covenant was better than the new, that the sacrifice of animals was superior to the sacrifice of Christ. Hence the author of

Hebrews reminds them that Christ's sacrifice brings final and definitive forgiveness. True cleansing of the conscience comes only through the blood of Jesus Christ, for his once-for-all sacrifice brings believers into the very presence of God.

What I find interesting is that falling away in Hebrews would mean returning to the law and Old Testament religion. Let me put it another way: Hebrews 11 is not just an aside in the book. It is not merely a chapter on the heroes of faith stuck into the book to inspire us. Quite the contrary. Hebrews 11 is integral to the message of Hebrews as a whole. Hebrews is a sermon (13:22), and like most sermons it has one main point. And that main point is "Don't fall away." The author calls upon his readers to persevere to the end. And how does Hebrews 11 relate to the main point of the letter? Because to persevere to the end, to keep following Jesus, means to keep trusting in God. The call to persevere is a call to faith. Falling away from Jesus—committing apostasy—occurs if one ceases to trust in God.

The strong warnings in Hebrews, then, are not legalistic. The opposite is the case. They are a summons to keep trusting in God. The author warns his readers about the peril of unbelief (Heb. 3:19). If someone were to fall away and fail to enter God's rest, that person would be returning to the law and the old covenant. But those who persevere do so because they believe; because they are trusting in God and in Christ's work on the cross instead of trusting in themselves.

I rejoice, therefore, in Brian Croft's book because he reminds us from Hebrews 11 (and 12) that Old Testament saints, and Jesus supremely, trusted in God. They persevered in faith even when their circumstances seemed to scream out that God's Word was untrue. Pastor Croft gives feet and hands to faith, showing us what it looks like in everyday life. May we follow those who have gone before us in faith, so that we, like them, will win an eternal reward.

Thomas R. Schreiner

James Buchanan Harrison Professor of New

Testament Interpretation, The Southern Baptist

Theological Seminary, Louisville, Kentucky, USA

Preface

I never wanted to be "one of those guys." You know: a pastor who schedules his next sermon series around his latest book deal. Even though this book you hold in your hand may suggest that I have compromised my convictions, let me give you a few reasons why I agreed to this project and have still maintained my fidelity in the matter.

The idea for this book wasn't even on the radar until after I had preached through the book of Hebrews. I loved preaching Hebrews. God was gracious in bringing forth much fruit from it in my congregation. However, there was a particular kind of fruitfulness from Hebrews 11 that was undeniable. Because of this, I thought that the Lord might be willing to use this section of this sermon series in the lives of those outside my church as well.

One of those marks of fruitfulness was the way our people came to a better understanding of the Old Testament characters in the Bible. We have several in our congregation who are either new Christians or Christians who did not grow up in the church, and their knowledge of the Old Testament was limited. Hebrews 11 proved to be one of the best places for these individuals in our church to learn about the Old Testament.

I was also amazed at the number of our folk who did not have a clear understanding that all the Old Testament works in unison to point us to Christ. This was best captured by the words of a very faithful, mature, and biblically proficient seminary student, who grew up in a faithful church yet still informed me, "I had never heard Hebrews 11 preached in such a way that demonstrates that its primary purpose is to point us to Christ." If this book in any way challenges someone's interpretive understanding of the Old Testament to consider Jesus Christ as the One to whom it all points, the work put into this book would be, without a doubt, worth it.

A final reason this book exists is my deep love for pastors and what I fear is a common missing link in the lives of many pastors and their ministries—endurance. Many young pastors today walk into unhealthy, dysfunctional churches and are quick to get discouraged and impatient, and to grow cynical and disillusioned; they either leave after a short time or simply bail out of pastoral ministry altogether. My hope is that the persevering faith to which the author of Hebrews calls every believer in Jesus Christ, despite suffering, trials, and difficulty in our lives, will be the same kind of enduring faith in which every shepherd of God's people will faithfully walk until the Chief Shepherd appears (1 Peter 5:4).

Whether you are a shepherd of Christ's people or simply a follower of Jesus Christ trying to press on, read this book as one who desires to demonstrate that you are a partaker of Christ (Heb. 3:14) and who longs to be met at the end by our King with these words: "Well done, good and faithful slave" (Matt. 25:21).

Brian Croft

Senior Pastor, Auburndale Baptist Church,

Louisville, Kentucky, USA

Introduction

Now faith is the assurance of things hoped for, the conviction of things not seen. For by it the men of old gained approval.

By faith we understand that the worlds were prepared by the word of God, so that what is seen was not made out of things which are visible.

Hebrews 11:1-3

It was 1914 when Ernest Shackleton and his crew boarded his ship to explore uncharted territory in Antarctica. The name of his ship was *Endurance*. He had no idea how ironic that name would be, as their ship became ice-locked and eventually was crushed to pieces—stranding them on floating ice for months. Shackleton and his crew, now facing impossible odds to survive and severe weather conditions, set out on a small boat to travel 800 miles to the nearest whaling station. Miraculously, they made it and sent a boat back to rescue the remaining crew. The most stunning reality about this entire drama is that in the midst of an ordeal which none should have survived, not one crew member lost his life. Although Shackleton's ship, *Endurance*, was crushed and sank into the frigid water, its name captures so powerfully why any of these men lived to tell this amazing story that has inspired millions.[1]

The message of Hebrews is likewise centered upon endurance. In Hebrews, what produces this endurance is clear: the writer exalts the supremacy and glory of Jesus Christ over all things. He accomplishes this purpose by vividly describing the glories of his Person and work. Jesus is God's Son through whom God supremely spoke, whom he appointed heir of all things, and through whom he made the world (1:2). Jesus is the radiance of God's glory and the exact representation of God's nature (1:3). Jesus is better than the angels (1:4) and Moses (3:3). He is the great, eternal, and faithful High Priest like Melchizedek (4:14; 6:20) who sympathizes with our weaknesses (4:15), mediates a better covenant (8:6; 9:15), and always lives to make intercession for his people (7:25). Jesus is also the perfect and sufficient sacrifice who through his blood purchased eternal redemption (9:12) from all our sins for all time (10:12, 18).

This glorious message about the sufficiency, supremacy, and glory of our Savior, High Priest, and King, Jesus, is designed to bring about one central outcome in the lives of God's people: endurance. Specifically, these truths are to motivate and empower the suffering and discouraged Christians to whom the author writes to endure in their faith in Jesus firm until the end, and not to fall back into their old life of Judaism.

The theological terminology of what the writer of Hebrews argues is "the perseverance of the saints" or "the eternal security of the believer." Wayne Grudem, in his systematic theology, defines the doctrine in this way: "The perseverance of the saints means that all those who are truly born again will be kept by God's power and will persevere as Christians until the end of their lives, and that only those who persevere until the end have been truly born again."[2] In other words, those who truly follow Christ will hold fast to Christ through struggles and hardships until the end. Those who remain faithful to the end affirm, by so doing, that they are true followers of Christ. Because of this, perseverance will be evident as they pay close attention to these truths (2:1), prove they are partakers of Christ (3:14), draw near with confidence to the throne of grace (4:16), press on to maturity (6:1), find forgiveness and eternal redemption (9:12), enter the holy place with confidence (10:19), draw near with a sincere heart in full assurance of faith (10:22), hold fast the confession (10:23), stimulate one another to love and good deeds (10:24), and encourage one another, while not forsaking regularly gathering together (10:25) or throwing away their confidence (10:35).

The endurance of faith in Christ's followers as a result of these magnificent realities about Jesus is the chief aim of the writer of Hebrews, and we find the first ten chapters powerfully promoting this purpose. This purpose does not change as the writer moves into Hebrews 11. In fact, the first ten chapters of Hebrews act as the foundations for understanding why the writer seems to interrupt his argument to refer back to these Old Testament saints. As we will see, Hebrews 11 acts as the template that truly exemplifies an enduring faith, and thus drives home the writer's purpose even more.

What is faith?

What is faith? If pressed to give a clear definition of faith, how would you respond? Could you respond? In Hebrews 11, the great faith chapter of the Bible, the author of Hebrews answers this question for us, giving a clear and succinct picture of what biblical faith looks like from the outset and how we persevere in it.

BIBLICAL FAITH IS THE ASSURANCE OF THINGS HOPED FOR (V. 1)

Faith is not a mystical power to be called upon when you want something. Neither are we exercising faith when we really hope for something which we actually doubt we will receive. Instead, faith is the assurance of the things we hope for which are promised to us by God in Christ. True, unshakable faith is founded on the certainty of God and supported by the testimony of the people of God throughout history.

First, the author of Hebrews tells us that "Faith is the *assurance* of things hoped for."[3] True faith is only true faith when what is hoped for is certainly going to take place. This stands in stark contrast to the view that faith is hoping for something which we doubt will actually happen. When your child has the stomach flu and you are desperately hoping that you will be spared from contracting it, this is not faith, because you have no grounds for assurance. You have no good reason to really believe you will be spared from getting sick. Unfortunately, this is often what our faith looks like.

Second, genuine faith is never in an object or circumstance; it is always in the one true God of the universe who reveals himself through the Scriptures. As Hebrews 1:1–3 teaches us, our faith is in the One who "spoke to the fathers in the prophets" and who now "has spoken to us in His Son." Also, because God's Son, Jesus, is the "exact representation" of the Father's nature, we actually come to know God the Father through knowing God the Son. Therefore, true faith must be directed solely toward our great God, whom we understand through the person and work of Jesus Christ.

Third, Hebrews tells us that by faith "the men of old gained approval" (11:2). The author means that the Old Testament saints gained approval through the same type of faith in which the author encourages his readers to persevere. In many ways, this verse serves as an excellent summary of the entire chapter of Hebrews 11, which in itself is a summary of many of the imperfect Old Testament saints who, despite their sins, doubts, and bad decisions, are lifted up as models of faith. The writer of Hebrews is not flattering these men and women of old. Instead, he is making the point that, in the midst of their sins, failures, and doubts, their approval before God came in the same way it does for all of us—faith in God and in his promises. Indeed, by looking at these Old Testament examples of faith, we see what true faith looks like.

In light of this truth, I must ask, do you possess genuine faith? Is your faith in the God and Creator of the universe, who in these last days has spoken to us in his Son? Or, upon examining yourself, do you find that your faith is in someone or something else?

This question is important because the answer determines whether we are forgiven of our sins and saved from coming judgment. As Ephesians 2:8 tells us, "[We] have been saved through faith." We escape God's wrath and receive eternal life through biblical faith in Jesus. Possessing biblical faith in Jesus means that we know for certain that Jesus lived a perfect life, died on the cross in the place of sinners, physically rose from the grave, and now reigns at the right hand of God, interceding for us as our great High Priest.

Of course, Christians must be careful to avoid certain pitfalls regarding faith. First, we must fight the temptation to redirect our faith toward other things. For example, in difficult circumstances, we must avoid the tendency to hope that everything will turn out fine in the end. Things do not turn out fine in and of themselves; rather, God orchestrates all things for his people's good and his own glory. Therefore, he is the one who merits our faith and trust; he is the explicit object of true faith.

Second, we must seek to maintain our commitment to God's will being accomplished, rather than to what we hope is God's will. How often we are disappointed when it turns out that God's will was not anything like we thought it would be! When God tells his people to "rejoice always" (1 Thes. 5:16), he intends for us to rejoice even during the deeply traumatic episodes of life.

Finally, we need to guard against even the symbols of our faith. The cross is not the object of our faith; the object of our faith is the One who hung on the cross. The Bible is not what we trust in; we are to trust in the Word of God, Jesus Christ, as recorded in the Bible. As Christians, we must make sure that the symbols of our faith never become the objects of our faith.

Biblical faith is the conviction of things not seen (vv. 1–3)

Faith is also a conviction of the certainty of the things we hope for that we cannot see. Very little faith is required of you if I tell you to sit in a chair, promising that the chair will hold you. You can look at the chair, examine the chair, and come to the conclusion that the chair is strong before taking a seat. However, if I tell you to sit down in an invisible chair, this requires a great deal of faith. Yet the author of Hebrews tells us that exercising faith means having confidence in the things which are unseen.

First, Hebrews 1:3 tells us that "by faith we understand that the worlds were prepared by the word of God." Contrary to some scientific theories, creation screams that there is a Creator. This is the testimony of the entirety of Scripture, and Paul says that the existence of God is evident to all because of the testimony of the creation around us: "For since the creation of the world [God's] invisible attributes, His eternal power and divine nature, have been clearly seen, being understood through what has been made, so that they [God-haters] are without excuse" (Rom. 1:20). Therefore, the writer to the Hebrews is saying, every star in the sky, every blade of grass, every flower, every strange and beautiful animal, as well as every unique human being—all testify to the reality of a glorious Creator, even though we cannot physically see this Creator with our eyes.

Second, faith is not just seeing creation and knowing the reality of our Creator, but also knowing that this Creator created the world through his Word (Heb. 1:3). The writer of Hebrews is telling us that there were no heavenly assembly lines and factories full of angels laboring hard to create the world. God, in all his power and glory, simply spoke the universe into existence. As *The Big Picture Story Bible* says, God spoke with "strong words. Powerful words," and was the sole architect of the universe.[4]

True faith believes that the powerful words from God that created the universe are the same words we find in the Bible, and that these words awaken our lifeless souls. Therefore, faith believes God's Word when it says all through Genesis 1, "God spoke ... and it became." Faith believes what the author of Hebrews opens his letter by saying: "God, after He spoke long ago to the fathers in the prophets in many portions and in many ways, in these last days has spoken to us in His Son, whom He appointed heir of all things, through whom also He made the world" (1:1–2).

Third, Hebrews tells us that we understand by trusting. Ultimately, genuine faith is progressively attained. First, we see. Second, we believe what God's Word says about what we see. Finally, we trust in God, who is not seen. This progression is implied in the last part of 11:3: "By faith we understand that the worlds were prepared by the word of God, so that what is seen was not made out of things which are visible." The truth we need to grasp is that God uses what is seen to move us toward belief in what is not seen.

Therefore, faith is not faith if it does not require belief in what we cannot see. It is not hard to have faith that God will provide for your needs when you have large sums of money in the bank. It is not knowing where and when monetary provision will come that requires faith. It does not require faith to wonder what the outcome of your sickness will be when the medicine you take is guaranteed to work. It is when your prognosis is uncertain that faith is required.

If faith is the conviction of things not seen, and if the men of old gained approval by their faith, we can conclude that God's intention for faith is to glorify himself. Faith shows our need of God; therefore, human boasting is excluded. If God works out his purposes—chief of which is glorifying himself—through human faith, why are we so surprised when God places Christians in circumstances in which the exercising of great faith is required? In these circumstances, our faith is tested and we are taught endurance. Christians need not resent the call of God upon them for a strong, enduring faith.

As we will see, Hebrews 11 is full of men and women who gained their approval in those moments when great faith was required. Because our true and enduring faith demonstrates that we belong to Christ, we should not resent such moments of uncertainty. Instead, we should embrace them and believe in God's promises for us in Christ. We must believe that God has ordained these circumstances so that we may prove our faith to be genuine and "may receive what is promised" (10:36).

Enduring ...
like Abel,
Enoch,
and Noah

By faith Abel offered to God a better sacrifice than Cain, through which he obtained the testimony that he was righteous ... By faith Enoch was taken up so that he would not see death; and he was not found because God took him up; for he obtained the witness that before his being taken up he was pleasing to God. And without faith it is impossible to please Him, for he who comes to God must believe that He is and that He is a rewarder of those who seek Him. By faith Noah, being warned by God about things not yet seen, in reverence prepared an ark ... and became an heir of the righteousness which is according to faith.

Hebrews 11:4–7

Who is the person who has taught you and impacted your faith in Christ more than anyone else? You might think of a parent, a pastor, or a friend who discipled you early in your Christian life. Regardless of who it was, you are probably thinking of someone who was alive at the time he or she taught you. However, while we may not think about it, we are also often taught by those who are long dead. We often learn from the great Christians of the past such as Augustine, Martin Luther, or Charles Spurgeon. Through figures such as these, we are inspired to persevere in the faith. Although they died long ago, they "still speak." In Hebrews 11, the author highlights the faith of many saints from the Old Testament. Just as we find inspiration from men such as Augustine or Spurgeon, so the writer desires that in light of the great faith of these saints, we too will be inspired to exercise great, enduring faith in Christ.

We have already seen from Hebrews 11:1–3 that faith is "the assurance of things hoped for, the conviction of things not seen." True faith is a faith in God and his promises to us in Christ. Though God is unseen, he is real and should be the sole object of our faith. The rest of Hebrews 11 offers example after example of those throughout Israel's history who gained approval from God because of their faith in looking for what God promised. In this chapter, we begin with the first three examples: Abel, Enoch, and Noah.

Evaluate our hearts before God (v. 4)

First, we are taught that we must evaluate our hearts before God. We find this lesson in the first recorded conflict after the fall of Adam and Eve (Gen. 4). In this account, two brothers, Cain and Abel, brought an offering to the Lord. The Lord accepted Abel's offering, but he did not accept Cain's. Strangely, the Genesis account does not give us any explanation as to why God accepted only one brother's offering. However, the text does reveal that Cain held jealousy in his heart against his brother, and afterward killed Abel. The author of Hebrews sheds further light on the hearts of these two brothers.

We are told that God valued Abel's sacrifice because Abel gave "a better sacrifice than Cain" (v. 4). Abel was a shepherd and Cain was a farmer, but the text does not tell us that it was the contents of each brother's offering that had anything to do with its acceptability or otherwise. Instead, the difference in the offerings was not in what was seen, but in what was unseen—the desires of each man's heart. Ultimately, the motives of these two brothers were quite different.

The author of Hebrews tells us that Abel offered his sacrifice "by faith." As such, the writer implies that Abel sought to bring his offering to God out of faith and trust in the Lord. In contrast, the text suggests that Cain brought his offering to the Lord thinking that his sacrifice was sufficient. As a result, the writer implies, Abel was declared righteous by his faith, coming away with a "righteous testimony" from God himself. This righteous testimony still speaks to challenge us to pursue God with the same faith that Abel had.

Thus, we can conclude that an enduring faith is one that realizes that God desires his people to have right motives and desires. Therefore, if we desire to persevere in our faith in God, we must evaluate our hearts before the Lord. This evaluation must take place for two reasons. First, because God knows our hearts. God knows everything which we seek to hide from others—our thoughts, intentions, motives, and desires. Just as God could see directly into the hearts of Cain and Abel and knew who brought his offering in faith, so God sees our hearts. Therefore, we must constantly evaluate our hearts and confess to the Lord any sinful motives or desires which we find.

Second, God is pleased through our efforts to serve him only when these efforts are done in faith. Through his offering Abel sought to honor God because of his love for him, while Cain did not. The application for the Christian life of this tale of two brothers is that our attitude in worship impacts whether or not our efforts to serve God are pleasing to him. God is not satisfied with our mere physical presence in a worship service. Instead, our attempts at worship are pleasing only when they are conducted by faith.

However, this does not mean that we will not struggle with our motives. As we struggle for pure motives in our worship, let us not forget that our efforts are acceptable to God only because of Jesus and what he has accomplished. Therefore, our faith in him and a desire for him to be exalted should be our greatest motivations during worship. We need to be constantly evaluating our hearts before the Lord so that our worship and service to him are done in faith, out of our love for him, and for his honor and glory.

Live to please God (vv. 5–6)

The second faith lesson relates to the mysterious figure of Enoch. Specifically, the author hopes that his readers will embrace the necessity of following in the footsteps of Enoch by living to please the Lord. The author makes two observations about living a life pleasing to the Lord.

First, in verse 5 we see that the reason Enoch was able to live to please the Lord was because he possessed faith. Through his faith, Enoch obtained the witness that "he was pleasing to God." Enoch walked with God, but apparently it was his faith in God that caused him to walk in a manner that pleased the Lord.

Second, in verse 6 the author argues that we are to live in

light of this example. As the author says, "Without faith it is impossible to please [God]." In order to please God, we must possess the faith of Enoch; specifically, we must believe that God exists, that he is who he claims to be, and that he rewards those who seek him (v. 6).

In order to accomplish this, we need to evaluate our aspirations. Do you aspire to live a life which is pleasing to the Lord? Or do your aspirations revolve around receiving the praise of your boss, friends, professors, or church family? We need to evaluate every area of our lives: family, work, educational pursuits, and other relationships. We must ask ourselves, "Am I conducting myself in a way that is pleasing to the Lord?"

The best way to accomplish this is to place road markers throughout our day where we ask this question. For example, during lunch or break times at work we should ask ourselves, "Have I pleased the Lord with my work and interactions with others thus far?" Ask yourself once dinner is over, "Have I pleased the Lord with my attitude toward my spouse, children, or roommates today?" After serving in some capacity at church ask, "Did I please the Lord with my attitude, motives, and interactions with others?"

If we honestly answer these questions, we will consistently find ourselves falling short. However, our deep-rooted sin is the reason why all this must be done "by faith," for in faith we come to God, knowing that he is the One who rewards those who seek him. Like Abel and Enoch, we please the Lord not when we do everything right, but when our natural instincts are to act in faith, knowing that the one true God of the universe has saved us through the perfect sacrifice of Jesus. Therefore, let us be reminded to cling to our Savior by faith.

Walk in fear of God (v. 7)

Whether or not a child possesses a good and healthy fear toward his or her parents is something that cannot be hidden. The way our children respond to our instruction gives clear evidence of whether they possess a healthy fear of our punishment. In the same way that a child fears his or her parents, we, as God's adopted children, are to have a healthy fear of God; whether or not we have this healthy fear is demonstrated by the way we respond to his instructions. In this section of Hebrews, the author exhorts his audience to look to the example of Noah and see how true faith manifests itself in a healthy fear of the Lord.

First, we know from Genesis 6 that God warned Noah that he would destroy the earth because of the great wickedness of humanity and that he commanded Noah to build an ark so that he would be rescued from this coming judgment. Second, we see that Noah responded in godly fear. As Hebrews 11:7 tells us, Noah, "in *reverence* prepared an ark for the salvation of his household." Despite any ridicule which Noah may have experienced from building an ark on dry land, Noah's healthy fear of God led him to do "all that God commanded him" (Gen. 6:22). Ultimately, Noah responded in faith to God by obeying his command to build the ark, and by acting upon this faith Noah was declared righteous by God.

As Christians, we become "heir[s] of the righteousness which is according to faith" in the same way as Noah—through faith in God and his promises. Yet men like Noah looked forward by faith to the promise of a coming redemption. However, we are fully accepted by God when we look back and see Jesus Christ. Through turning from sin and placing our faith in Jesus, our sins are forgiven and we receive Jesus's righteousness. Salvation should never be divorced from a godly fear of judgment, however. Just as Noah responded to God's instruction because of a healthy fear of God's judgment, so we Christians need this healthy fear of God and the reality of his judgment upon sin in order to appreciate fully our need to obey God's commands.

Regarding endurance, at least two ramifications of walking in a healthy fear of God should be present in our lives. First, walking in the fear of the Lord should give us a great zeal to share the gospel with those who are still in rebellion against God. The question should not merely be, "When was the last time you shared the gospel with someone?" Instead, a better question in evaluating our own personal fear of God is this: "When was the last time your motivation for sharing the gospel was because you were burdened by the fact that this person stands condemned by a holy God and faces eternal judgment?"

Second, walking in the fear of the Lord should cause us

to take our sin seriously. When we sin, we should run to the mercy of God and cling to the righteousness of Christ. When we take our sins lightly, we deceive ourselves into thinking that God takes sin lightly as well. Thus we fail to walk in fear of the judgment which we would most certainly face apart from the finished work of Christ. Though we are saved from this judgment, we must not allow ourselves to forget the reality of it, for it will move us to endure in our faith.

The lives of these men of old teach us what an enduring faith looks like for Christians. Therefore, let us be diligent to evaluate our hearts, live to please the Lord, and walk in a healthy fear of the Lord, for these are means by which we continue in our enduring faith in Christ.

Reflect on these points

1. *"God knows everything which we seek to hide from others—our thoughts, intentions, motives, and desires. Just as God could see directly into the hearts of Cain and Abel and knew who brought his offering in faith, so God sees our hearts." Reflect on your motives and desires.*

2. *"We need to evaluate every area of our lives: family, work, educational pursuits, and other relationships. We must ask ourselves, 'Am I conducting myself in a way that is pleasing to the Lord?' ... If we honestly answer these questions, we will consistently find ourselves falling short." Reflect on the reality that we cannot please God in any area of our lives without acting out of faith in Christ.*

3. *"In the same way that a child fears his or her parents, we, as God's adopted children, are to have a healthy fear of God; whether or not we have this healthy fear is demonstrated by the way we respond to his instructions." Reflect that a healthy fear of God is good, and consider in what ways it helps you to endure in your faith.*

Enduring ...
like Abraham

By faith Abraham, when he was called, obeyed by going out to a place which he was to receive for an inheritance; and he went out, not knowing where he was going. By faith he lived as an alien in the land of promise … for he was looking for the city which has foundations, whose architect and builder is God. By faith even Sarah herself received ability to conceive … since she considered Him faithful who had promised. Therefore there was born even of one man, and him as good as dead at that, as many descendants as the stars of heaven in number, and innumerable as the sand which is by the seashore … By faith Abraham, when he was tested, offered up Isaac … He considered that God is able to raise people even from the dead, from which he also received him back as a type.

Hebrews 11:8–12, 17, 19

Although I do not have one, I know that many people have developed a dependence on their GPS to get them where they want to go. Can you imagine how frustrating it would be if your GPS started to play tricks on you and stopped in the middle of nowhere, refusing to tell you where to go? Or if the GPS told you just to drive south and keep traveling for an undisclosed period of time? We would hate to travel that way because we want to know where we are going all the time; following such guidance would require a tremendous amount of trust in our GPS—a trust most of us do not have in mechanical devices.

In the story of Abraham, however, we see a man who is forced to travel in this way. He is told to leave his home and "just go." However, it is not an ancient GPS system that is leading him. Instead, the one commanding Abraham to go is God himself. Yet Abraham obeyed God, and the writer of Hebrews tells us that Abraham obeyed because of his great enduring faith.

Trust in God's guidance (vv. 8–10)

The Christians receiving these words in Hebrews would have been very familiar with the importance of Abraham. They would have known that he was the central figure in Israel's history. In the Old Testament, the account of the life of Abraham begins at the end of Genesis 11, revealing his lineage and that he was married. Yet what begins to unfold is the account of how God worked through Abraham (who at this point was still called Abram) to create and establish his chosen people, Israel. Ultimately, Abraham was the one through whom the Savior and Redeemer of the world would come.

The account of Abraham is centered on a promise that God made with Abraham when the latter was at the youthful age of seventy-five. God said, "I will make you a great nation, and I will bless you" (Gen. 12:2). However, Abraham and Sarah had no children at this point. The first command God gave Abraham was to "go forth from your country, and from your relatives and from your father's house, to the land which I will show you" (12:1). Abraham was confronted with the first of many circumstances in which he needed to trust in the Lord and his promises through obedience. This tension is what the author of Hebrews references regarding Abraham's life and why he is an example of faith for us.

The account in Genesis 12 shows Abraham's obedience to the Lord in doing all that was commanded. In Hebrews 11:8 we find that Abraham left "by faith," trusting in the Lord to guide him. In this statement, the author of Hebrews is already challenging us, "Would you do this?" Would you sell your house, move all your belongings, place your children in the car, say goodbye to your parents, and start driving—all the while not knowing where you are going? Although Abraham experienced many bumps in the road as he journeyed, the writer of Hebrews highlights that Abraham had faith because he obeyed when the Lord called him to go, even though he did not know where he was going.

Even after Abraham arrived at the land promised by God, the writer of Hebrews says that he still lived there as "an alien" (11:9). This appears strange to us. We define an alien as someone who is dwelling in a place that is not their home, but this was the land which the Lord had promised to give Abraham. God later acknowledged to Abraham that this land was an inheritance for the generations to come after him— the great nation to come from him. Yet we find that not only Abraham, but also the generations after him (Isaac and Jacob) lived as aliens in this foreign, yet promised, land. They too sojourned in this way "by faith" (v. 9).

The writer of Hebrews reveals to us that the faith Abraham had in God was not just in the promise of land, or even in the promise of a child in old age, but in the heavenly reality of these promises. Hebrews 11:9–10 says that "by faith" he was "looking for the city which has foundations, whose architect and builder is God." Hence, the "alien" status Hebrews gives Abraham came as a result of him realizing that the promise of God was one of eternal redemption that would be provided through his prized son, Isaac—the seed of whom was Christ (Gal. 3:16).

Abraham is mentioned as an example of faith because he lived his days on this earth in faith that God would guide him through the circumstances of life and lead him to the heavenly city. Abraham's life is, therefore, strangely similar to ours as Christians—sojourners in places which are not our real homes. Hence the apostle Peter identifies the recipients of his first letter as "those who reside as aliens, scattered ..." (1 Peter 1:1). As Christians, our calling is the same as that of Abraham. We are to live as residents of the heavenly city and by faith trust that God will guide us through our time in this foreign land.

We therefore need to ask ourselves, "Is this how I view my life as a follower of Christ?" You are an alien placed here for a short time to declare the gospel of Jesus and the glory of God in a dark place among spiritually blind people. But maybe you have become quite comfortable here? Perhaps you love your stuff and the pleasures this place provides. As a result, you do not miss your true home much anymore.

I had a missionary friend who left for the field with a great zeal to take the gospel to that very dark place. A common danger for missionaries who go to a completely different culture is that of getting sucked into the pagan culture they have entered. Sadly, this is exactly what happened to my friend; he was completely ineffective as a gospel witness to this nation. In light of this dangerous tendency, we must continually evaluate our comfort level in this foreign land, for if we get sucked into the comforts of this world too much, we will be completely ineffective in performing that which God has called us to while we reside as sojourners.

In this connection, I cannot help but think of John Bunyan's classic book, *The Pilgrim's Progress*. This is an allegory of the Christian life in which the main character, Christian, faces all kinds of challenges which seek to divert him from his journey to the Celestial City. The whole book is about this man's persevering faith as he struggles along his journey to the city which is his true home.

As Christians, this is our task. By faith, we live as foreigners in a strange land, looking for the celestial city. While in this strange land, we must trust the Lord to guide us through our struggles, difficulties, sufferings, and unexpected turns. The reason we can do so is because we know that God uses them all to display the gospel of Jesus through our enduring faith.

Depend on God's provision (vv. 11–12)

The promise of land was accompanied by the promise that Abraham's wife, Sarah, would have a child, even though she was long past childbearing years. Imagine being in your eighties and God telling you that finally you will have a child.

Any lady past childbearing years will appreciate how this must have struck Sarah, yet we find that she responded as Abraham did: "by faith" (v. 11). In verses 11–12, we find three reasons why both Abraham and Sarah responded in faith.

First, our minds are flooded with the many obvious implications of a ninety-year-old woman having a child. We can assume that the most obvious implication to Abraham and Sarah was that this was physically impossible. However, in accomplishing his purposes, God often uses means that make it undeniable that he alone is at work. Trusting in God at this moment required great faith, which we find Sarah possessed; for she "received ability to conceive, even beyond the proper time of life" (Heb. 11:11).

Second, Sarah had faith that the impossible could be possible because of the One who made the promise. "She considered Him faithful who had promised" (v. 11). Her faith was not in how she rationally figured out that this could happen. Instead, she had faith in God and trusted in the One she knew to be faithful. Later, God was faithful to Sarah in giving her a son, Isaac.

Third, God's promise to Abraham was not just for one child, however, but for "as many descendants as the stars of heaven in number, and innumerable as the sand which is by the seashore" (v. 12). God promised a great nation through which all nations would be blessed. The writer of Hebrews implies that Abraham ultimately had faith that God was promising that a Redeemer would come from this great nation. As the apostle Paul wrote,

> Even so Abraham believed God, and it was reckoned to him as righteousness. Therefore, be sure that it is those who are of faith who are sons of Abraham. The Scripture, foreseeing that God would justify the Gentiles by faith, preached the gospel beforehand to Abraham, saying, "All the nations will be blessed in you." So then those who are of faith are blessed with Abraham, the believer.
>
> (Gal. 3:6–9)

The promise of God to Abraham was not just land, but a heavenly city to which he was an heir through faith. Similarly, the provision and promise of God to Abraham was not just a child and a great nation, but that the Redeemer would come from that nation.

We know that this Redeemer was Jesus, the Son of God. Therefore, the promise to Abraham was ultimately the gospel. The promise that "all the nations of the earth" would be blessed refers to the fact that those from every people group who turn from their sins and place their faith in Jesus are reconciled to God and become heirs of the heavenly city.

As Christians, our calling is to live by faith as Abraham and Sarah did. Abraham made many bad decisions because of his impatience and doubts, yet he is lifted up as a model because he had faith in God and his promises. Let us be children of Abraham, walking as aliens by faith, depending upon the provision of our Savior, and ever looking for our inheritance in that heavenly city.

Obey God's commands (vv. 17–18)

The year was 1986. I was twelve years old. The play was *The Wizard of Oz*. It was a requirement for sixth-graders to participate in the school play. I was terrified because nothing scared me more than the idea of having to sing, act, and dance in front of people. I was so troubled about this that I took it upon myself to meet with the teacher overseeing the play and plead for mercy. I pled for the worst stagehand job; I desperately did not want to sing, act, or dance. When she agreed not to give me a role which required any singing or dancing, I left her, feeling relieved and confident. I said these foolish words to myself: "If she honors her word [no singing or dancing], surely there is nothing she would ask me to do that I could not do."

Well, she honored her word—no singing or dancing. However, I was given the role of the Wizard—one of the most important and difficult speaking parts in the entire play. I had to pronounce words which I had no idea even existed. I hated every minute of this experience and I am hopeful that the recording of this play has been destroyed. If it has not, I am confident it will be when Jesus returns and makes "all things right." Perhaps you have not been manipulated into playing a role in a play like this, but I assume each of us has said something very similar to what I said to myself: "Surely this will never be asked of me."

Returning to Abraham, we know that God asked much

from Abraham and his faith. Many years went by as Abraham waited for the promised son to be born. Finally, when Abraham reached the age of one hundred, his son, Isaac, was born. If we were Abraham, knowing who this child was and what he represented, we would be tempted to say, "Whatever God asks of me in the future, surely it would never be something that would harm this child." Yet the writer of Hebrews tells us that this is exactly what God asked of Abraham. Obedience would require a true, real, and irrefutable faith.

One of the primary ways we can identify true faith in God and in his promises is when someone's life is marked by a willingness and desire to obey what God has commanded, regardless of how insane or irrational that obedience might seem to the world. Abraham did not merely prove this, but he also set the bar high—as we see from these verses in which the writer mentions the account where Abraham was told by God to sacrifice his only son on an altar (Gen. 22).

Abraham's faith in God and his promises was tested and proven when he did what God commanded him in offering up Isaac (Heb. 11:17). His faith had been maturing and growing over the years. Yet this was the supreme test of his faith, because this command appeared to be a contradiction to the promise. While we would have been tempted to question God, Abraham is portrayed as simply obeying God.

We need to learn from the writer of Hebrews that true faith, like the faith of Abraham, will endure until the end. Faith cuts through our natural instincts which desire to question God's wisdom, use rational thinking, and demand that we have the right to approve or disapprove of how God chooses to work in our lives. A mark of a strong and powerful faith is that it cuts through all this, obeys God's Word, and simply trusts in him.

In light of what Abraham was commanded to do, we need to guard ourselves from ever making this foolish statement: "Surely God wouldn't ask me to do that!" Those who have actually said such words know how foolish it is to say that to a sovereign and wise God. I once said, "Surely God would not call me to be a pastor." On another occasion my wife told me, "Surely God won't call you to be a pastor." As I write this, I am now in my eighth year as senior pastor of Auburndale Baptist Church in Louisville, KY.

We should be wary of convincing ourselves that we know what God's plan is for our lives. However, there is a part of me that hopes that some readers might be foolish enough to say, "I'm older and entering the last years of my life; surely God won't ask me to be a missionary?" Or "That's a rough neighborhood; surely God won't ask us to move there?" Or "I just received this tax return; surely God won't have me spend this to care for others?" If you are foolish enough to say such things, I pray you will respond with great faith and obedience when God asks you to do those very things.

Believe in God's power (v. 19)

How often does our common sense and rational thinking steal our faith in God? How often do we forget that the One who created the universe by speaking it into existence is able to do far beyond whatever we could think? The writer of Hebrews once again points us to the faith of Abraham to challenge us that, if we trust God, we must trust in who God is and his great power to do whatever he chooses. It appears that Abraham obeyed God's command because he trusted that God was powerful enough to do the unimaginable (Heb. 11:19).

The reality is this: in order to have true faith, we must believe that God is able. This is what allowed Abraham to believe in God's purposes and trust in his power. Specifically, the writer says, "[Abraham] considered that God is able to raise people even from the dead." Some might say that this information does not appear in the account in Genesis, yet Abraham is recorded as telling the men who accompanied him, "Stay here with the donkey, and I and the lad will go over there; and *we* will worship and return to you" (Gen. 22:5).

Even though Abraham was taking Isaac as a sacrifice, Abraham still trusted that Isaac would return with him. We do not know if Abraham trusted that God would provide the animal—which he did (Gen. 22:13). The writer of Hebrews does state, however, that Abraham had faith that even if he did sacrifice Isaac, God was able to raise him from the dead. We often need to be reminded of this truth: God is able. Regardless of what you face today, God is able to do the unimaginable.

The writer of Hebrews hints that, to some degree, Abraham did receive Isaac back from the dead, which is what he means when he writes "from which he also received him back as a type" (11:19). Another translation says, "Figuratively speaking, he did receive Isaac back from death" (NIV). In other words, Abraham had already decided to obey the Lord and sacrifice his son, despite the Lord stopping him at the last second (Gen. 22:12). Therefore, in a sense, Abraham did receive his son back from the dead.

As we reflect on the way the writer of Hebrews describes the testing of Abraham, the mercy of God in the gospel should come to the forefront of our minds. God has truly accomplished the unimaginable—reconciling condemned sinners to a holy God through Jesus Christ. If we think about it, our enduring faith in Christ is a testimony of our belief that God can and does accomplish the unimaginable.

Reflect on these points

1. *"By faith, we live as foreigners in a strange land, looking for the celestial city. While in this strange land, we must trust the Lord to guide us through our struggles, difficulties, sufferings, and unexpected turns. The reason we can do so is because we know that God uses them all to display the gospel of Jesus through our enduring faith."* Reflect on the events of your life, knowing that God is at work, bringing you to the exact place he wants you to be.

2. *"As Christians, our calling is to live by faith as Abraham and Sarah did … Let us be children of Abraham … depending upon the provision of our Savior."* Reflect on your need for a Savior to rescue you from sin and

*judgment, and how God has fully made that provision
in Christ.*

3. *"In light of what Abraham was commanded to do, we
need to guard ourselves from ever making this foolish
statement: 'Surely God wouldn't ask me to do that!' ...
We should be wary of convincing ourselves that we
know what God's plan is for our lives." Reflect on God's
call and for us to obey him in faith, even when we do not
understand—and the blessing that follows such
obedience.*

4. *"How often do we forget that the One who created the
universe by speaking it into existence is able to do far
beyond whatever we could think? ... Regardless of what
you face today, God is able to do the unimaginable."
Reflect on God's power and that there is nothing he
cannot accomplish through you and in you.*

Enduring ...
like Isaac,
Jacob, and
Joseph

By faith Isaac blessed Jacob and Esau, even regarding things to come. By faith Jacob, as he was dying, blessed each of the sons of Joseph, and worshiped, leaning on the top of his staff. By faith Joseph, when he was dying, made mention of the exodus of the sons of Israel, and gave orders concerning his bones.

Hebrews 11:20–22

I was talking to my children about their great-grandmother, who had recently passed away. In the midst of the conversation, they asked some good questions about their "Gigi." One of their questions was, "How do we know that Gigi is in heaven with Jesus?" We had a great conversation about the gospel and we were all reminded that we must have faith in Jesus to go to heaven. Then I asked, "So how can we be sure that Gigi is in heaven with Jesus?"

I thought I knew what would come next: a statement acknowledging that they knew that Gigi believed in Jesus. However, to my surprise I heard this answer from one of my children: "Because when she was dying, I heard her asking Jesus to take her home." Even children see that a genuine faith is most evident when we demonstrate it in our darkest hour. As we now approach Hebrews 11:20–22, an enduring faith in death is the common link we find between the three "men of old" considered in this text.

Trust in God's sovereign calling (v. 20)

The doctrine of election is foundational for a right

understanding of our salvation and what it means to be adopted eternally into the family of God. The statement of faith of my church describes it this way: "Election is God's eternal choice of some persons unto everlasting life—not because of foreseen merit in them, but of His mere mercy in Christ—in consequence of which choice they are called, justified, and glorified."[1] In other words, God's election of his people is based not on their actions, but instead on the sovereign will of a just God. This doctrine has been known to make some people uncomfortable. However, I would suggest that the Bible consistently presents election as a means of strengthening the faith of Christians during difficult times, such as when they are facing death.

Isaac's blessing of his two sons points directly to God's sovereign calling of his people, and the author of Hebrews uses this blessing to motivate his readers to persevere in their faith. It is "by faith" that "Isaac blessed Jacob and Esau" (v. 20). This is referring to the events of Genesis 27, when Jacob deceived Isaac in order to receive the greater blessing from his father. Esau, the elder brother, was supposed to receive the greater blessing, but instead it was "mistakenly" given to Jacob. Despite the lies and deceit in the account, Romans 9 (as we shall see below) tells us that the choice of Jacob was actually predetermined by the sovereign purposes of God.

Hebrews tells us that this blessing was given in faith by Isaac (v. 20). He knew the promise given to his father, Abraham, and he knew that the son he blessed would be the one who would move closer to inheriting the promise of God. Genesis

27 shows Isaac's faith; once he realized he had blessed Jacob instead of Esau, he did not try to take the blessing back. Instead, he accepted the outcome as God's sovereign purpose in fulfilling his promise. Thus, even as Isaac approached his death, he demonstrated his faith in God.

The apostle Paul makes a similar point in Romans 9 when he discusses God's choosing of Jacob over Esau. Paul tells us that Jacob was chosen before these twins were even born—before either son had done anything good or bad. Why? Romans 9:11 says, "so that God's purpose according to His choice would stand." The clear teaching of Scripture is that God is the One who calls and awakens sinners to see their rebellion and need of a Redeemer.

How should this reality of God's sovereign calling help us to persevere in our faith? First, our election is designed to convince us of the security of our salvation. Charles Spurgeon said,

> I believe the doctrine of election, because I am quite sure that if God had not chosen me I should never have chosen him; and I am sure he chose me before I was born, or else he never would have chosen me afterwards; and he must have elected me for reasons unknown to me, for I never could find any reason in myself why he should have looked upon me with special love.[2]

When the doctrine of election is discussed, people often want to focus on those whom God does not choose; however, we often fail to consider our own election. When we do consider our election, we should be overcome with joy that God has secured our salvation through the life, death, and resurrection of Jesus. We did not deserve to be saved, and this mercy we have been shown should empower us to endure through the most difficult of circumstances.

Second, trusting in God's sovereign calling of his people should cause us to trust God when loved ones die and we do not know where they stood with Christ. Recently, one of our church members had plans to visit an elderly lady whom she cared for as part of her job. As part of this visit, which was planned for a Saturday, she and her husband hoped to read Scripture and pray with her. Unfortunately, the elderly lady died on the Friday night. Even though the church member had had previous discussions with this woman regarding the gospel, she was tempted to beat herself up for not going earlier. She was tempted to take responsibility for the state of this elderly woman's soul.

While there are many responsibilities we should feel as Christians, the spiritual state of a dying individual is not one of them. The reality of God's sovereign call to salvation is in the hands of our Creator and no one else. Does God use these circumstances to give us a greater urgency to share the gospel? Yes. Does God use moments like these to help us feel the weight of eternity and give us a greater zeal to want to be with people in their dying hour to remind them of the treasure of Christ? Absolutely. However, the responsibility of a person's soul is not ours to take, nor should we ever place an expectation like that on ourselves.

Hope in God's eternal promise (vv. 21–22)

Facing death seems to cut through all the insignificant matters of our lives. Life is never more real than at these moments. When we are with people on their deathbeds, we are reminded of how little our money and accomplishments matter in comparison with the important things in life. We need reminders such as these because we are prone to forget what really matters. The author of Hebrews gives us a similar reminder in the example of Jacob and Joseph when they were on their deathbeds.

In Hebrews 11:21 we see Jacob's faith in the face of death as he "blessed each of the sons of Joseph." This scene is found at the end of Genesis, where he blesses his sons, especially his two grandsons by Joseph (Ephraim and Manasseh), who would eventually become that great nation through whom the Messiah and Redeemer would come. This blessing affirms Jacob's belief in the promises of God given to Abraham, and is why Jacob worshipped on his deathbed, continuing to trust God for his unshakable promise and plan of the better country.

The last chapter in Genesis tells of Joseph's death and his dying request for his family to take his bones and bury them in the Promised Land. Remember that Joseph and his family were in Egypt when he died; this led to the enslavement of the Israelites by the Egyptians and God's eventual deliverance of the people through Moses. The author of Hebrews recognized that Joseph, by faith, "made mention of the exodus of the sons of Israel" through this request. We do not know how much detail regarding the coming exodus God revealed to Joseph, but we do know that Joseph had faith that God would be faithful to his promise and bring the Israelites to the Promised Land. As Joseph was dying, he was looking even then to that better, heavenly country. God's promise gave him the hope he needed to endure in his faith, even in death.

The writer of Hebrews uses these examples because the task of his readers was the same: to endure in their faith through suffering, persecution, and even death. For modern-day readers, the same task remains. If we are honest with ourselves, all of us have the desire to persevere in our faith, but we often question what we will do when we face death. The Puritans said that we must spend our entire lives preparing to die well. As Richard Sibbes said,

> To die well is not a thing of that light moment as some imagine: it is no easy matter. But to die well is a matter of every day. Let us daily do some good that may help us at the time of our death. Every day by repentance pull out the sting of some sin, that so when death comes, we may have nothing to do but to die. To die well is the action of the whole life.[3]

So the question remains: how can we prepare to die well? The answer is simple: we do exactly what these three men of old did—hope in God's eternal promises. These men hoped in God's eternal promises because they trusted God's Word. The remedy is the same for us. If we hope in God's eternal promises, we will have all the faith we need to persevere and remain firm until the end, not shrinking back—even in our darkest hours.

What trial do you face today that is shaking your faith? Regardless of whether your trials involve work, health, marriage, family, sin, or anything else, if you are a believer in Jesus Christ, the eternal promises of salvation which God has given you are enough for you to remain faithful to Christ, both in life and in death. May God build our faith in these eternal promises as we look to treasure the One who purchased us and made all of these promises a reality for us—Jesus Christ.

Reflect on these points

1. *"When we ... consider our election, we should be overcome with joy that God has secured our salvation through the life, death, and resurrection of Jesus. We did not deserve to be saved, and this mercy we have been shown should empower us to endure through the most difficult of circumstances." Reflect on God's great mercy in calling you from darkness unto salvation.*

2. *"Facing death seems to cut through all the insignificant matters of our lives ... When we are with people on their deathbeds, we are reminded of how little our money and accomplishments matter in comparison with the important things in life." Reflect on God's heavenly promises that are fully ours in Christ.*

Enduring ...
like Moses

By faith Moses ... was hidden for three months by his parents, because they saw he was a beautiful child; and they were not afraid of the king's edict. By faith Moses ... refused to be called the son of Pharaoh's daughter, choosing rather to endure ill-treatment with the people of God than to enjoy the passing pleasures of sin, considering the reproach of Christ greater riches than the treasures of Egypt; for he was looking to the reward. By faith he left Egypt, not fearing the wrath of the king; for he endured, as seeing Him who is unseen. By faith he kept the Passover and the sprinkling of the blood ... By faith they passed through the Red Sea ...

Hebrews 11:23–29

I have a friend who, many would say at one time, had it all. He was young, wealthy, respected, well known, and could have had anything he wanted in this world. You can imagine how everyone reacted to the news that he was leaving his lucrative job to go to seminary and pastor a small church in Kentucky. You may be thinking the same thing many in his life thought: "What would possess you to make such a decision?" I believe that his answer would be very similar to what the writer of Hebrews records in Hebrews 11:23–27, where he speaks of Moses and his enduring faith.

In the previous chapter we saw that Christians can and should persevere in their faith even to the point of death. In this chapter, we will see that the writer of Hebrews desires to communicate to Christians that a persevering faith in Jesus is marked not just by how we leave this world, but also by how we live in this world. According to the writer, there may be no greater person to learn this from than Moses. I pray that, as Christians, we would learn from Moses how to demonstrate a persevering faith that will stand through suffering and persecution, and also stand against the allurements and temptations of this world.

Fear God, not man (vv. 23, 27)

The first main point that the writer makes in referencing Moses' enduring faith is the faith demonstrated by his parents in disregarding the king's evil decree. Think back to the beginning of Exodus and the king's edict: "Kill all the male babies of the Israelites." If you were found to conspire against the king in regard to his ruling, you would certainly be killed. Yet Moses' parents hid him because "he was a beautiful child" (v. 23). This is not a reference to Moses' cuteness, but rather to his parents' recognition of God's hand and purposes upon his life. Moses' parents saw that he was unique. However, recognizing Moses' beauty was not enough to quench their fear of disobeying the king's edict; Moses' parents did not fear the king because, on account of their faith, they held a greater fear of disobeying the Lord.

Later, we read that Moses soon came to adopt the faith of his parents, and, like them, feared God more than the king. Moses left his high standing in Egypt as a prince in order to be with his people, who were under Pharaoh as oppressed slaves. Specifically, Moses abandoned the comforts of Egypt and endured hardship because of the One "who is unseen"

(v. 27). That phrase should take our minds back to Hebrews 11:1, where faith is defined as "the assurance of things hoped for, the conviction of things not seen."

We can imagine what an encouraging word this must have been to the original readers of Hebrews. These people, who were tempted to shrink back from the faith because of their fear of man, would have known about and admired Moses. The same dangers tempt us today. Fear of man is a dangerous mindset that not only will make us miserable, but, as the writer of Hebrews highlights, can also easily quench our endurance in the faith.

What are some of the ways in which fear of man can paralyze our faith? First, fear of man shows up when we are driven to please people. While there is nothing wrong with wanting to make others happy, we are often motivated to do things to please people rather than God. Ironically, this is most evident in my life as a pastor. When I do something because I think my congregation wants me to do it, even though I should be spending my time doing something else, I am fearing man more than God, and this is sin.

Second, fear of man happens when we care more about what other people think of us than about what God thinks of us. How often do we do something or say something (or *don't* do something or *don't* say something) because we are worried about what someone might think of us? One example is when we pray in front of others. If you pray in a church service and you are more focused on what others think of your prayer than on what God thinks, you are fearing man more than God in that moment.

The point is that our lives can quickly and subtly be consumed with fearing man more than God. What is the solution? Ultimately, the problem of fear of man is largely an issue of focus. When we are convinced that man has greater power, authority, and control over us than God, our fear of man has blinded us to the truth. God is the one who controls our eternal destiny. God is the one who created, sustains, and rules over man. As such, it only makes sense to fear God over man.

Treasure Christ, not the world (vv. 24–26)

If one simple phrase could define a true, enduring follower of Jesus it would be this: to treasure Christ, not the world. The apostle Paul put it this way when writing to the suffering Philippians: "I count all things to be loss in view of the surpassing value of knowing Christ Jesus my Lord, for whom I have suffered the loss of all things, and count them but rubbish in order that I may gain Christ" (Phil. 3:8). Although Moses was looking forward in faith, we find in him the same affections and perseverance which should mark all true followers of Jesus.

The writer of Hebrews shows us several ways Moses' decision to leave Egypt serves as evidence that he was rejecting the riches and comforts of this world for Christ. It was "by faith" that when Moses was an adult, he "refused to be called the son of Pharaoh's daughter" (v. 24). Most people would have done anything to be recognized as the son of Pharaoh's daughter and receive the privileges, honor, power, and treasures of Egypt (v. 26). Moses, however, not only left this comfortable life, but also left in order "to endure ill-treatment with the people of God" (v. 25). In essence, Moses left the royal family to become a slave.

Why would Moses do this? Moses left the royal family because he recognized the greater inheritance he would receive through the promised Redeemer to come. As such, "he [considered] the reproach of Christ greater riches than the treasures of Egypt" (v. 26). Moses was able, with eyes of faith, to look beyond all that was happening to him in the present and look forward to see the value of the Christ to come. He looked forward to the reward that Christ would provide, and he knew that his present suffering was no match for the glory that would one day be his.

If Moses was able to have such a persevering faith by looking forward to see the treasure and value of the coming Christ, how much more should we as Christians be able to look back and see the treasure that is our Savior, High Priest, and King? We are able to look back and see the Redeemer who was promised to Moses, whereas Moses was only able to anticipate.

For believers, the question we must answer is this: What are you tempted to treasure and value more than our glorious Savior, High Priest, and King? We must ask this question because all of us are tempted every day to treasure something worthless from this world more than Jesus. We do so because we lose sight of his unspeakable value and the value of the coming reward. Whether we are tempted by possessions, money, status, comforts, or something else, we must guard ourselves from such horrible deception by pressing on, just as Moses did, in the faith.

Trust in God, not in yourself (vv. 28–29)

Moses' faith not only caused him to fear God (as opposed to the king) and treasure Christ (as opposed to the treasures of Egypt), but also assisted him in obeying God, in order to spare the Israelites from the final plague upon Egypt. The setting of this scene is as follows: Moses has gone to Pharaoh telling him to let the Israelites go, but Pharaoh has refused. Pharaoh continues to refuse, even though God sends plague after plague to demonstrate his great power over Pharaoh. The final plague is now coming: God is about to kill all the firstborn in the land of Egypt.

In order to prevent the Israelites from experiencing this plague, the author of Hebrews tells us that Moses "[sprinkled] the blood" from a slaughtered lamb on the doorposts of their homes. When the angel of death came, he passed over these homes, protecting all those staying in them. This event established the "Passover" celebration. As the Passover was celebrated annually, God's people were reminded of God's great judgment that came upon Egypt and the deliverance that they received due to Moses' faith and obedience to God's instructions.

Likewise, we, the new-covenant people of God, are to look back with eyes of faith upon our Passover lamb, Jesus, who perfectly obeyed God's instructions and in doing so bore the sins of his people and provided the righteousness God requires. Our enduring faith is, therefore, identified when we rely and trust not in ourselves, but in Christ, who is our "righteousness, and sanctification, and redemption" (1 Cor. 1:30).

Moses demonstrates faith in Christ which endures through the struggles, trials, and hardships of this world; a fear and trust in God that caused him to treasure Christ more than anything else. In whom are you trusting and what are you treasuring today?

Reflect on these points

1. *"Fear of man is a dangerous mindset that not only will make us miserable, but, as the writer of Hebrews highlights, can also easily quench our endurance in the faith." Reflect on how much you fear man compared with your fear of God.*

2. *"All of us are tempted every day to treasure something worthless from this world more than Jesus. We do so because we lose sight of his unspeakable value and the value of the coming reward." Reflect on what you treasure most in this world and how it compares with Christ.*

3. *"Moses demonstrates faith in Christ which endures through the struggles, trials, and hardships of this world; a fear and trust in God that caused him to treasure Christ more than anything else." Reflect on your tendency to trust in yourself. When are you most prone to do so?*

Enduring ... like Joshua and Rahab

By faith the walls of Jericho fell down after they had been encircled for seven days. By faith Rahab the harlot did not perish along with those who were disobedient, after she had welcomed the spies in peace.

Hebrews 11:30–31

When you were a child, did you ever do something helpful for your parents with the motive of manipulating them in order to avoid their punishment? I can remember being especially helpful to my parents when I had done something wrong but did not know if they knew about it. Sure enough, my dad seemed always to know what I had done. However, with what seemed to be a sick, sinister enjoyment, he would allow me to continue in my pleasant behavior. He would lead me to think I had slipped something by them, only to then let me discover that he knew it all along. Of course, I would then receive my punishment.

When we read the story of Rahab in the book of Joshua (ch. 2), we may be tempted to think she had a similar motive when she allowed the spies sent from Joshua to stay with her. She knew that Joshua was coming with his army to conquer, and she saw an opportunity to save herself by being nice to the spies. Yet, as the writer of Hebrews makes known to us, Rahab was spared not in spite of manipulative tactics, but because of her enduring faith which she had in God and his mercy. Before we learn from Rahab, however, Joshua himself also teaches us how to endure in our faith.

Rely on God's great power (v. 30)

Following the life of Moses, Joshua sought to lead God's people into the Promised Land. On their quest, they found the city of Jericho, which was surrounded by massive, impassable walls. Yet God told Joshua to do something which on all human accounts seemed incredibly foolish. He was to have the people march around the walls with trumpets for seven days. As the author of Hebrews tells us, Joshua obeyed in faith, and upon the completion of the seven days of walking, "the walls of Jericho fell down." Through Joshua's faith exercised in obedience, God displayed his great power and chose to do the unimaginable: delivering Israel's enemies directly into their hands.

We can assume that the persecuted Christians receiving this letter would have been tempted to think from these examples that God would deliver them from the persecution they were receiving because of their faith in Jesus. Yet faith can also bring about the opposite. Nevertheless, Christians do experience deliverance, but it is a deliverance from our greatest enemy—Satan. In his letters Peter describes Satan as "your adversary, the devil, [who] prowls around like a roaring lion, seeking someone to devour" (1 Peter 5:8). Our physical enemies are no match for this enemy, whose attacks upon God's people are relentless. Yet he has no power over us. Why?

Satan has no power over us because God, in his great power, has defeated this enemy through the life, death, and resurrection of Jesus. The power of the gospel has forever delivered us from Satan's power, and although the devil still prowls around, looking to devour, he has no hold over us. Yet how often do we gripe about those who treat us badly, say mean things to us, and provoke us, though these annoyances are not worthy to be compared with the victory we have from the enemy of our souls? Think about how ridiculous it is for us to sing of how we will glory in our Redeemer, only to fall back into thinking about how "this guy drives me crazy for saying things behind my back." When we realize that God has delivered us from our worst and most powerful enemy, all our physical enemies should pale in comparison.

This would have been an important word for the discouraged and suffering Christians who originally received this letter. Perhaps they were discouraged because they had an expectation that, through faith, God would deliver them from their persecution; in reality they should have been encouraged to press on in the faith because God had already delivered them from their greatest and most powerful enemy. As Christians, we must realize that the same could be said of us. Perhaps that physical enemy you face looks so great and harmful because you have lost sight of the victory over the Destroyer, who was defeated at the cross on your behalf. Although your physical enemies may never go away, if you focus on that ultimate victory you will receive the grace you need in order to deal with your physical enemies in a gracious and loving way that honors Christ.

Trust in God's great mercy (v. 31)

As Joshua was making plans to enter and conquer the Promised Land, he sent two spies into the land to scope it out. This is where we first meet a very unlikely character: a woman named Rahab. Not only did she welcome the spies, but she actually hid them in her home and protected them from certain harm. Because she did this "by faith" (v. 31), God showed her mercy and allowed her and her family to be spared once Joshua invaded the land. Although she was not a Jew, she became one of God's people, lived with Israel from that day on, and became part of the direct genealogy of Jesus (Matt. 1:5). Finally, the author of Hebrews tells us that her faith demonstrated God's power to do the miraculous.

Notice how the writer of Hebrews introduces Rahab: "By faith *Rahab the harlot* did not perish along with those who were disobedient." I don't know about you, but I tend to introduce people in this way: "This is Cara, my wife." Or "This is Samuel, my son and oldest child." We tend not to introduce people as prostitutes. Either the writer of Hebrews is really mean-spirited, or he wants us to see something very significant to encourage us to endure in our faith. As a prostitute, Rahab would have been one of the most ostracized and shunned women in the land. Yet, because of her faith in God and his mercy, she and her family were spared from the certain judgment and death to come.

How is this to encourage believers in Christ? Though faith is required, God does it all. Rahab was the person most undeserving of God's mercy, yet she received God's blessing, even becoming part of the Messiah's genealogical ancestry. She had faith in God, and God did the unimaginable. We are like Rahab: we were helpless to do anything to save ourselves except act in faith that God would show mercy to those who did not deserve it. Thankfully, we received such mercy when God poured out his wrath on his Son, who stood condemned in our place.

Although it is God who does all the work, in order to receive this salvation we must respond to this good news in a faith that endures through the suffering, difficulties, and uncertainties of life. We must respond with a faith that demonstrates that we have been shown mercy and have not been treated as our sins deserve.

What difficulty do you face that makes you doubt God's mercy to you? I ask the question in this way because is this not how we usually react to suffering? When trouble comes, we ask, "Where is God?" and we doubt his mercy toward us. Even if you find yourself in the darkest of days, these dark days have not changed the mercy which God has shown you in Christ. Because of this, allow the certainty of God's mercy to us in Christ to empower your endurance.

Reflect on these points

1. *"Satan has no power over us because God, in his great power, has defeated this enemy through the life, death, and resurrection of Jesus. The power of the gospel has forever delivered us from Satan's power, and although*

the devil still prowls around, looking to devour, he has no hold over us." Reflect on the power of Christ in the victory we have from our greatest enemy.

2. *"Rahab was the person most undeserving of God's mercy, yet she received God's blessing, even becoming part of the Messiah's genealogical ancestry. She had faith in God, and God did the unimaginable. We are like Rahab." Reflect on the mercy of God in that we have not been treated as our sins deserve.*

Enduring ...
through
soaring and
suffering

And what more shall I say? For time will fail me if I tell of Gideon, Barak, Samson, Jephthah, of David and Samuel and the prophets, who by faith conquered kingdoms, performed acts of righteousness, obtained promises, shut the mouths of lions, quenched the power of fire, escaped the edge of the sword … Women received back their dead by resurrection; and others were tortured, not accepting their release, so that they might obtain a better resurrection; and others experienced mockings and scourgings, yes, also chains and imprisonment. They were stoned, they were sawn in two … being destitute, afflicted, ill-treated (men of whom the world was not worthy), wandering in deserts and mountains and caves and holes in the ground.

And all these, having gained approval through their faith, did not receive what was promised, because God had provided something better for us, so that apart from us they would not be made perfect.

Hebrews 11:32–40

How do you explain why some faithful Christians always seem to face difficulties, while others never seem to face trials? For example, why do some Christians have bright and talented children, while others have children with learning disabilities? How do we make sense of this? Should we conclude that God is rewarding faithfulness to some more than to others?

Some would say, "Yes." In fact, some would even say these differences are due to some Christians having a greater faith than others. Those who are not trusting God are punished, while those who do trust God are rewarded. Fortunately, the writer of Hebrews addresses this wrong thinking through one of the most stunning contrasts in the entire Bible.

Endurance through soaring (vv. 32–35a)

If we are honest with ourselves, we consider the victorious soaring events of our lives to be normal. Although we live in a fallen world in which everything is tainted with sin, we somehow still expect our lives to be easy and comfortable. When life does not work out that way, we often find ourselves questioning God. This is why, when we have those moments of victorious soaring, we must make sure that we have a proper and humble perspective.

The author of Hebrews illustrates the importance of maintaining such a proper perspective. Beginning in verse 32, he lists various people throughout Israel's history who qualified for the "hall of faith," such as Gideon, David, Samuel, and the prophets. He then supplies a list of events, which are also intended to serve as a summary. These events are not related merely to the few individuals he mentions, but are intended to encompass everyone who has "gained approval through their faith" in God and his promises (v. 39).

Many of these mighty acts, such as shutting the mouths of lions and seeing the dead resurrected, would even be considered miracles. In these, we see examples of God doing the miraculous through the enduring faith of his people. Other events mentioned include conquering kingdoms and performing mightily in war. As you read the text, you may rightfully be thinking of other examples from the Old Testament. These situations also serve as examples of soaring victories that happen because of God's great power at work in persevering faith.

There is, however, a danger as we contemplate these particular examples. I have great concern when we view our lives through a tainted lens, quoting as our favorite Bible passages those verses which point us to soaring through life. Quite frankly, that is not a realistic way to look at life. When we focus our lives on such expectations, we can easily begin to feel entitled to these victories.

On the other hand, we learn that these soaring victories may come because of our persevering faith in Jesus, as shown in this portion of Hebrews 11. As God was accomplishing his purposes through his people, he was doing great things to display his character and ways to the world. The key is to remember that God may choose in his goodness and grace to allow us to experience these soaring victories. When he does, our response needs to be one of humility and gratefulness, not entitlement and self-praise. Thus, if you experience success after success in your job, continually remind yourself of God's gracious plan of using you in your success to make him known. If your child grows up to have great intelligence, do not conclude that you are an excellent parent. Instead, conclude that you serve a kind and generous God who rewards faithfulness.

When the soaring victories come into your life, experience them humbly, knowing that you have done nothing to deserve them and that they have not come by your hand. Also, experience such victories cautiously, knowing that they are not the norm. If you receive these soaring victories through your enduring faith, give God all the honor and praise. When you do this, you will maintain a biblical perspective which will prepare you for when suffering comes.

Endurance through suffering (vv. 35b–40)

We are all tempted to stop reading at the end of verse 35a because these verses capture our expectation of God; but as we continue reading we find that many of those who are celebrated in Hebrews because of their enduring faith did not receive such soaring victories. Instead, on account of their faith they were persecuted, tortured, imprisoned, and martyred (vv. 35b–38).

Can you imagine the mental and emotional anguish that comes with imprisonment, mistreatment, and martyrdom? This anguish would certainly resonate with the suffering Christians who first received this letter, as we know from Hebrews 10 that many of them were experiencing many of these discomforts (though not yet martyrdom) and found themselves discouraged, not understanding why they were suffering while others soared.

My favorite collection of audio lectures is a series of biographical talks given by John Piper on various Christians throughout history who suffered greatly yet remained faithful to Christ until the very end. The title of this series is "Men of Whom the World Was Not Worthy." This title is taken from Hebrews 11:38. While anyone can have a persevering faith when soaring, far fewer demonstrate perseverance when suffering. However, notice that only those who suffered for their faith are given this distinction. Those who have enduring faith in Jesus despite horrific suffering have proven that their faith is real and genuine.

Do you see why the heretical health-and-wealth prosperity gospel message is so harmful? The message that Jesus will make you healthy, give you success at work and in the home, and help you reach your inner potential is wrong. Such a message not only feeds our innate feelings of entitlement in this world, but is also antithetical to the biblical call to follow Jesus, which is to deny yourself and take up your cross (Mark 8:34). While we may soar at times, the call to the true, biblical gospel is a call to suffer.

We must be prepared to suffer for the Lord's name's sake. Peter says, "If you are reviled for the name of Christ, you are blessed" (1 Peter 4:14). The message of the New Testament is not just that the call to follow Jesus is a call to persecution, but that though we receive persecution on account of the name of Jesus, we are actually blessed to represent the name of Jesus to a world which hates him. Many of us do not experience this persecution often, but we need to recognize that Christians all around the world do. Let us always remember to pray for the persecuted church and be challenged by the faith of those who suffer for Christ's name. Furthermore, let us be willing to suffer in the same way.

We must also be prepared to suffer in general, knowing that

Christ is most magnified in the suffering of his people, as we depend upon him for comfort and strength while striving to remain faithful. How else can we answer the hard questions of "Why does a young mother with young children get diagnosed with multiple sclerosis?" or "Why does that athletic middle-aged man get rheumatoid arthritis?" I would suggest the reason is this: Christ's worth and glory are most clearly seen *through those who suffer and yet remain faithful to him*. When suffering comes, God is working out his purposes and wants to use *us* to display him to those who experience our joy, satisfaction, and trust in our Savior at those times.

We must be prepared to suffer because Jesus suffered on our behalf. He was innocent, yet he suffered scourging, mocking, ill-treatment, and the most inhumane death. He suffered and died, bearing the full wrath of God as punishment for our sins—all so that we would not face such wrath and that our sins would be forgiven. If Jesus suffered in this way to save us from our sins, we must heed the words of Charles Simeon, who, at the end of a life filled with suffering, said to his friend Joseph Gurney,

> My dear brother, we must not mind a little suffering for Christ's sake. When I am getting through a hedge, if my head and shoulders are safely through, I can bear the pricking of my legs. Let us rejoice in the remembrance that our holy Head has surmounted all His suffering and triumphed over death. Let us follow Him patiently; we shall soon be partakers of His victory. [1]

Whether we soar or suffer throughout our lives, we do so looking to the promise. We soar, realizing that the greatest earthly victory pales in comparison with the glory to be revealed. We suffer, knowing that our suffering is for but a moment, while the reward for our persevering faith will last forever. This is the point the writer of Hebrews makes at the end of this chapter, hoping that it will be an encouragement to these suffering Christians.

Although everyone mentioned in Hebrews 11 "gained approval through their faith," they still did not "receive what was promised" (v. 39). All of these faithful individuals died looking forward to their great reward (salvation), which could not be received until Jesus came and purchased it with his own life. Now that he has done this through his life, death, and resurrection, all those of faith (both those in Hebrews 11 and us) will receive the reward and be made perfect together on that day when Jesus returns for his people.

Therefore, as Christians, whether we soar through the victories of life that God grants us or we are given the great privilege of suffering for Christ's sake, let us recognize that both soaring and suffering come in the mysterious providences of God. Both soaring and suffering come to test and prove our faith in Jesus, and, ultimately, both soaring and suffering come so that Christ's name and glory will be displayed to the world. Regardless of what we experience, may we demonstrate our great enduring faith through trusting in Jesus, believing with certainty that the great reward which has been promised to us is certain because of the suffering which Jesus endured.

Reflect on these points

1. *"God may choose in his goodness and grace to allow us to experience these soaring victories. When he does, our response needs to be one of humility and gratefulness, not entitlement and self-praise." Reflect on the grace of God when he gives us soaring victories in life.*

2. *"Christ's worth and glory are most clearly seen through those who suffer and yet remain faithful to him. When suffering comes, God is working out his purposes and wants to use us to display him to those who experience our joy, satisfaction, and trust in our Savior at those times." Reflect on the sovereign purposes of God that are at work in our suffering.*

3. *"Whether we soar or suffer throughout our lives, we do so looking to the promise. We soar, realizing that the greatest earthly victory pales in comparison with the glory to be revealed. We suffer, knowing that our suffering is for but a moment, while the reward for our persevering faith will last forever." Reflect on how both soaring and suffering in life causes you to look forward to the promises of God in Christ.*

Enduring ...
because
of Jesus

Therefore, since we have so great a cloud of witnesses surrounding us, let us also lay aside every encumbrance and the sin which so easily entangles us, and let us run with endurance the race that is set before us, fixing our eyes on Jesus, the author and perfecter of faith, who for the joy set before Him endured the cross, despising the shame, and has sat down at the right hand of the throne of God.

For consider Him who has endured such hostility by sinners against Himself, so that you will not grow weary and lose heart.

Hebrews 12:1–3

Recently, a fifty-two-year-old member of our church, who suffers from arthritis, ran a mini-marathon with a time of two hours and seven minutes. You may be thinking, "Wow, for an old guy, that's pretty good!" Or maybe you are thinking, "Wow, for a young buck, that's pretty good!" Either way, you perceive it to be an impressive accomplishment. This member has run several of these races over the years and it is interesting to hear him describe the experience. He trains hard for the race months beforehand, usually dropping between ten and fifteen pounds for the race. He eats well, drives his wife crazy obsessing over the upcoming race, and is ready to go the morning it comes.

As the race goes on, some people take off while others begin to drift back. This church member runs a steady pace, knowing what he must do to finish the race in the best time he can. While he feels pretty good most of the race, the pain intensifies around the ten-mile mark. In order to finish the final few miles, he must overcome many physical and mental obstacles. And although he is always shooting to make it in less than two hours, he usually comes up just short of that goal. Nonetheless, he is always encouraged by the accomplishment.

Whether you run mini-marathons or only run if someone is chasing you, we all need to understand the dynamics of such a race because this is how many of the New Testament writers, including the author of Hebrews, describe enduring the Christian life. The faithful saints of Hebrews 11 have instructed us in many ways about how we persevere in our faith. However, each of the examples of Hebrews 11 that makes up the "great ... cloud of witnesses" (12:1) contributes to the climax of the writer's argument in the first three verses of Hebrews 12. As we consider Hebrews 12:1–3, we need God to expose where and why we might be growing weary in our faith and to show us how to "run with endurance the race that is set before us."

Lay aside stumbling blocks (v. 1)

I have always enjoyed watching shows like *American Gladiators*, where two contestants are forced to run races against each other, often with a twist. They have to maneuver around big blocks and obstacles, being sprayed with water hoses, and, most importantly, figure out how to escape the clutches of a strong gladiator, all the while seeking to cross the finish line first. In such a race, speed alone will not get you to the finish line. Instead, the person's ability to fight through the stumbling blocks is the key to achieving success.

This is the kind of race being described in the opening verses of Hebrews 12. The Christian life is a race that is full of stumbling blocks, obstacles, and large gladiators who desire to knock us back to the starting gate. In particular, the author of Hebrews points out two main stumbling blocks in the Christian race: distracting encumbrances and sin. Distracting encumbrances are things in a Christian's life which, though not necessarily sinful, are unhelpful and which keep us from running the race well. We must lay aside these encumbrances and also the sin in our lives which causes us to stumble throughout the race.

The obvious question which we must ask ourselves in responding to such a text is, "What are the encumbrances and sins which are holding us back in our race?" The answer is going to be different for each of us. One sin that so easily entangles me is self-sufficiency. I often try to rely on myself and my own strength instead of on God and his grace. Whichever sins most frequently entangle you, lay them down at the foot of the cross, knowing that they have been dealt with by Jesus. Confess your sin and press on in the race, knowing that there is forgiveness.

Let us also lay aside those things which, though not inherently sinful, hinder our spiritual growth as Christians. For some, this may be obsessing over their favorite sports teams or spending hours on social-networking Web sites.

While such things are not sinful in and of themselves, we must ask ourselves whether our affections for these things help us run the race or hinder us.

Run the race (vv. 1–2)

As already mentioned, the Christian life is a race that we are exhorted to run: "Let us run ... the race" (v. 1). The writer of Hebrews uses the race analogy because it teaches us how to live and die well.

Our life is a race that has a beginning (our conversion) and an ending (our death). At the end of the race, we will receive our heavenly reward and spend eternity with Christ. The difficulty comes with the race itself. At times, we are going to run well. At other times, we will experience pain and setbacks, either through obstacles along the course itself or personal baggage. During these times, we will often wonder if we will even finish the race. Our success, therefore, depends upon running with endurance and with our eyes set upon Jesus.

First, let us run with endurance. One wonderful truth about running is that the more you run, the stronger you are the next time you run. While getting prepared for a mini-marathon is difficult, the fact that you run one week builds your endurance and enables you to run more strongly the next week. This analogy corresponds directly with the Christian life: our endurance as Christians comes from living as Christians. I have had Christians tell me all the time that in their discouragements they feel they are going backwards, and yet, when the darkness passes, they seem to run better than they did before. We are to run with endurance, and the best way to build endurance is to just run the race as best you can. If you cannot run, walk. If you cannot walk, crawl. As long as we make daily progress, the endurance will come.

Second, in addition to running with endurance, we must persistently fix our eyes on Jesus as we run. No better exhortation exists for discouraged Christians than the call to fix our eyes upon Jesus. If you do not understand why something has happened to you, fix your eyes on Jesus. If you cannot shake a certain sin, fix your eyes on Jesus. What aspect of Jesus are we to fix our eyes on? Fix your eyes on the fact that Jesus is "the author and perfecter of faith" (v. 2).

Why fix our eyes on Jesus? Because through Jesus's life, death, and resurrection, we can know that the prize for the race has already been won—purchased through his sufferings. The prize has already been won; we just have to finish the race. As Christians, we do not need to finish the race first or in a certain time; we simply need to finish well, honoring the One who purchased the prize for us through his own life.

Consider Jesus (v. 3)

How often do we consider and dwell on our struggles, uncertainties, and circumstances, instead of fixing our eyes on Jesus and what he has accomplished on our behalf? The writer of Hebrews tells us that we need to consider two aspects of Jesus's Person and work if we desire to persevere in the faith and not grow weary.

First, we must consider Jesus's joyful suffering. Although

Jesus was the perfect God-Man who never sinned, he endured the pain, suffering, and shame of a brutal execution. In addition, Christ also experienced the full wrath of God as he suffered the punishment for our sins. Jesus endured this judgment on our behalf so that we would not have to face it. Now Jesus calls us to suffer for his name's sake; we must look to him and his example to endure joyfully through our own suffering.

Second, we must consider Jesus's eternal reign. After enduring the shame of the cross, Jesus sat down at the right hand of the throne of God. Jesus joyfully endured suffering because he knew the victory that would be purchased as he was raised from the grave. Now Christ rules with authority over all the nations and over all our circumstances. Ultimately, this is the message of Hebrews: consider him who suffered for us, was raised, now rules in all his supremacy and power, and is now our great, sympathetic High Priest before the Father, interceding on our behalf.

As Christians, the answer to persevering in the faith is clear: consider Jesus. Consider Jesus as the author and perfecter of our faith. Consider his joyful sufferings that purchased our salvation. Consider that Jesus is reigning even now over all things and interceding for us before his Father. No matter what your struggle is, consider Jesus. As you do so, you will find the endurance to run the race well.

Reflect on these points

1. "Whichever sins most frequently entangle you, lay them

down at the foot of the cross, knowing that they have been dealt with by Jesus. Confess your sin and press on in the race ... Let us also lay aside those things which, though not inherently sinful, hinder our spiritual growth as Christians." Reflect on the stumbling blocks in your life and what you are doing to remove them.

2. *"At times, we are going to run well. At other times, we will experience pain and setbacks ... During these times, we will often wonder if we will even finish the race. Our success, therefore, depends upon running with endurance and with our eyes set upon Jesus."* Reflect on how well and faithfully you are running the race that has been set before you.

3. *"As Christians, the answer to persevering in the faith is clear: consider Jesus."* Reflect on the hope of Christ and how his person and work are enough to spur us on to endure.

A final word
to pastors:

Implications for
endurance in
pastoral ministry

Remember those who led you, who spoke the word of God to you; and considering the result of their conduct, imitate their faith ...

Jesus ... that He might sanctify the people through His own blood, suffered outside the gate. So, let us go out to Him outside the camp, bearing His reproach ...

Obey your leaders and submit to them, for they keep watch over your souls as those who will give an account. Let them do this with joy and not with grief, for this would be unprofitable for you.

Hebrews 13:7, 12–13, 17

Let's face it: pastoral ministry is hard. You may be reading this final word, questioning whether you will hold fast through the discouragements, struggles, dealings with difficult people, and trials that await you every time you darken the doors of your church. Hopefully, this word on the heels of the message of this book will spur you on to persevere through the struggles and gladly spend yourself for Christ, his gospel, and his people. The book of Hebrews is arguably the clearest book from which to learn endurance in our faith, and the faith of pastors is no exception.

Let us not forget the purpose of the writer of Hebrews, which is to exalt the supremacy and glory of Jesus Christ over all things, a foundational truth that is enough to empower the most discouraged Christian to hold fast his or her faith until the end. As demonstrated earlier, this purpose is powerfully accomplished in the first twelve chapters of Hebrews.

Then we come to chapter 13, the last chapter, and here the writing shifts into a list of exhortations for these Christians to walk in, demonstrating that they are enduring in their faith in Jesus. Striking implications for us as pastors and for pastoral ministry are found in this final chapter, and they should encourage us, not just in our faith, but also toward steadfastness in our ministries until the Chief Shepherd returns. In particular, three powerful reminders should cultivate endurance in any faithful shepherd of the Lord Jesus Christ—regardless of the discouragements and sufferings he might face.

Remember those who spoke the word of God to us (vv. 7–9)

I'll never forget one late-night conversation I had with one of my pastoral mentors. I was at the end of the interview process at Auburndale and the church had invited me to come and preach in view of a call. My mentor had asked me a series of thoughtful questions, paused, and then said, "Well, I have affirmed your gifts, I have taught you everything I know; go pastor that church and know I will be praying for you." There was much wrapped up in those words, but the unspoken message was, "I have taught and invested in you, and I am counting on you, with God's help, to be faithful and a good steward of what you have been taught." I regularly think about those words, and it is just another reason I desire to be faithful to endure. Words like these should be a reason *you* desire to endure in your ministry too.

This first exhortation written to these Christians— "Remember those who led you ..."—implies that pastors are where they are today because someone first spoke the Word of God to them, taught them, and invested in them. Because of this, pastors are now in the privileged position, as preachers of God's Word and shepherds of God's people, to do the same regularly in their people's lives.

First, this word was spoken to us by these people's words: "Remember those … who spoke the word of God to you." In this context, the primary identity of "those who led you and spoke the word of God" is the leaders within the churches of these Christians. The Christians addressed in Hebrews are to affirm that the teaching of these pastors and leaders was sound and true.

The writer implies that "those who led" taught "Jesus Christ … the same yesterday and today and forever" (v. 8). Wrapped up in one verse we see that Jesus, the Son of God and great High Priest, has always existed, eternally reigns as King, and is unchanging. What a great summary of this entire book whose aim is to exalt Jesus as supreme over all things! The doctrinal statement of verse 8 sets the tone for the argument of verse 9, where the writer makes clear what these teachers didn't teach: "Do not be carried away by varied and strange teachings." Some of these Christians were tempted to forsake their faith in Jesus because of persecution, but there was also the temptation to go back to Judaism and their old way of life. Perhaps they were questioning their faithful leaders' teaching and were drawn to the teaching of false teachers in their midst who were trying to enforce the Old Testament law on Christians, specifically aspects involving foods (v. 9). The writer exhorts them to remember those who led them faithfully by speaking the Word of God through exalting Christ and exposing false teaching.

Second, the word was spoken to us by these leaders' deeds. There is a popular saying, "Preach the gospel at all times, and if necessary use words." Although intended to encourage faithful gospel living, this saying is negatively used to justify non-assertiveness in sharing the gospel. However, the gospel is preached with words; without words, the gospel is not preached! Yet we do need to acknowledge an important truth in this popular saying. The message of the gospel is affirmed by consistent holy living and faith. For this reason, the writer says about these leaders who spoke the word of God to the Christians, "Considering the result of their conduct, imitate their faith" (v. 7).

The writer tells them to remember those who led them and spoke to them because the holy conduct and enduring faith they modeled affirmed the truth of the gospel. There is a strong implication that if these Christians were to reject those who led them well, faithfully spoke God's Word to them, and powerfully lived it out before them, they would also be rejecting their faith in Christ.

The message is clear that those who previously spoke the Word of God to us were a gift from God that is to be treasured. As pastors, we of all people should recognize and be most grateful for so many who, by God's sovereign grace, were placed in our lives to lead us faithfully, speak God's Word to us, and live lives that we should imitate. That is what the writer hopes this instruction will accomplish in them and, consequently, in us as we look back on our lives and think of those who spoke God's Word to us in both word and deed.

Take a moment to think about these people in your life. Think of that person who shared the gospel with you and led you to trust in Christ. Think of that seminary professor who made a special investment in you. Think of that parent or grandparent who labored faithfully to teach God's Word to you, despite it being at a time when your heart was cold toward it. Think of that pastor who, week in and week out, faithfully spoke the Word of God to you and lived that Word out in his life.

During the coming week, contact those who have had this kind of impact in your life. I know that I am not alone in feeling that the most meaningful encouragement I receive is not from something that happened this past week, but hearing from someone whom I discipled ten years ago, who benefited from me speaking the Word of God then.

As you remember those who led you and spoke the Word of God to you, be thankful to God that, as an extension of his sovereign care of you, he placed a faithful parent, pastor, Sunday-school teacher, or friend in your life to help you persevere in your faith in Jesus. God used these people to bring you to the place of spiritual maturity you find yourself in today. Their investment in us also prepared us for the ministry to which we have been called and find ourselves in today.

Also, remember that we pastors are now the leaders (v. 7). We are those called to this task (the gift from God to our people), not just to speak God's Word to our people, but also to live that Word out in our daily lives before them. Feel the honor of being in this position, but also the seriousness of it. Is there something in your life that is glaringly inconsistent with the gospel you proclaim and the Word you teach? May this awesome responsibility before God and those who spoke God's Word to us motivate us to faithfulness, purity, and endurance, regardless of the difficulties we may face in our churches.

Remember what it means to follow Jesus (vv. 10–16)

Our materialistic, consumer-driven culture has greatly confused the true, biblical call to follow Jesus. However, the writer of Hebrews reminds us of it as he begins the next set of exhortations. The exhortations seem to run together in this section, but the flow of thought by the writer takes an obvious turn in verses 9–10. As he describes how these leaders faithfully spoke the Word of God to the Christians, specifically in the warning against strange teachings (v. 9), he begins to do something he has done frequently in this book: he references the old covenant, the old sacrificial system, their old way of life, to demonstrate why Jesus, the better sacrifice and mediator of a better covenant, is superior. From this, the clear call of the gospel and what it means to follow Jesus is revealed.

Following Christ means to go "outside the camp." The writer

paints the picture of the old sacrificial system (vv. 10–11) in which the high priest would sacrifice certain animals and bring their blood into the holy place (v. 11) as an offering for sin. The body of that slain animal was then taken outside the camp and burned (v. 11). The "therefore" in verse 12 refers back to that old sacrificial system to demonstrate that it was a shadow of what Jesus accomplished in perfectly and completely atoning for sin through his sufferings and death on the cross.

In order that he might sanctify and redeem his people, Jesus "suffered outside the gate" (v. 12), a reference to the location of Jesus's crucifixion outside the gates of the city of Jerusalem. This is similar to the place outside the camp where the sacrificed animals, whose blood was the offering for sin, were taken. From this amazing picture comes the call to follow Jesus: "So, let us go out to Him outside the camp, bearing His reproach" (v. 13). This is an echo of Jesus's words: "If anyone wishes to come after Me, he must deny himself, and take up his cross and follow Me" (Mark 8:34).

Dear brother and fellow pastor, when you went to pastor your church, did you think that there wouldn't be difficult people, discouragements, and hostility to the gospel? When you find yourself in the fire, are you tempted to say, "Hey, this is not what I signed up for"? The writer of Hebrews says that the call to follow Jesus is to go "outside the camp, bearing His reproach." How much more relevant is that for each of us who shepherds, sacrifices, and leads those who follow Jesus? If our calling is to lead God's people to follow Jesus faithfully, it requires jumping to the front of the line and taking them outside the camp. When we wallow in our difficulties and discouragements because they are hard (and they really are sometimes), I don't think we realize that we are telling our people to go outside the camp (where Jesus is) while we hang back.

As the trials and discouragements come, pay close attention to the instruction "Let us go ... outside the camp" (v. 13). Why? Because that is where Christ is: "Let us go out to Him." If we are to follow Jesus faithfully and lead his people to do the same, we must go where Jesus goes. He is outside the camp; therefore, that is where we must joyfully go, regardless of the cost. How are we able to follow him to that place? Because "here we do not have a lasting city, but we are seeking the city which is to come" (v. 14). When as a pastor you face the most painful difficulties, betrayals, and sufferings, remember that this is what it means to follow Jesus and shepherd his people. May that knowledge empower every pastor to rest in Christ, continually offer a sacrifice of praise to God (vv. 15–16), and thus endure in his ministry.

Remember that we will give an account to God for souls (v. 17)

It is amazing how much we have succumbed to evaluating our ministries and our effectiveness as pastors on the basis of numbers. I hope we all want to see more and more people hear the gospel, follow Jesus, and be baptized. I hope we all want to see more people come to our churches and hear God's Word preached and to experience the loving fellowship of our people.

Yet I am concerned that our preoccupation with numbers has caused us to miss the nature of our primary biblical task as pastors—to shepherd the eternal souls of God's people.

The nineteenth-century Scottish pastor and trainer of pastors John Brown wrote a letter to one of his students newly appointed over a small congregation and extended this word to him:

> I know the vanity of your heart, and that you will feel mortified that your congregation is very small, in comparison with those of your brethren around you; but assure yourself on the word of an old man, that when you come to give an account of them to the Lord Christ at his judgment seat, you will think you have had enough.[1]

Pastors are to keep watch over souls. This is clearly seen in this exhortation to these Christians to "Obey your leaders and submit to them" (v. 17). The reason they are to obey and submit to their leaders is because the leaders "keep watch over" their souls. This idea of "keeping watch" is similar to that of a soldier who stands on a wall and tirelessly guards that wall from the enemy. Why are these Christians to obey and submit to their leaders? Because their leaders are commanded to watch over their souls just as a soldier would guard a wall with alertness, protection, and care. This is what it means to shepherd God's people.

The responsibility to care for the souls of others is tremendous; and just when we think it couldn't get any weightier, we find this comment: "They keep watch over your souls as those who will give an account" (v. 17).

I can remember the pressure and burden I felt when I realized that I would answer to God for tending not just to my own soul and the souls of my family, but also to the souls of the people of my church. In my first few years as the senior pastor of Auburndale Baptist Church, I lay in my bed at night unable to sleep because this burden was so great. There are all kinds of reasons why our church moved to a plurality of pastors in 2006, but this exhortation may be the most significant. The burden and responsibility for the souls of people and the need to give an account to God for them is too great for one man to carry alone. However, though the burden is great, the amount of joy received in carrying out this responsibility is designed by God to be equally great. This is why the writer says, "Let them do this with joy and not with grief."

Pastors, let us not forget that our calling to keep watch over the souls of our people is a great, joyful burden that is unlike anything else we experience. It will and should consume us. It should keep us up at night. It should burden us like nothing else can. Until we feel the weight of that burden and embrace it, we will not experience the tremendous joy that comes from that burden. Not all pastors embrace it, but those who do so and spend, sacrifice, and exhaust themselves for Christ and his people—we know the unique joy and grace that God gives in it. It is that joyful burden to give an account before our God for the souls of our people that should give us pause whenever we are tempted to take it lightly and inspire us to endure through the difficulties.

We have a divine call to press on faithfully in this work, knowing that the Chief Shepherd, Jesus Christ, will judge and reward our ministries when we stand before him. I dare say, dear brother, it will not be based on attendance records or any other worldly standard. Instead, it will be the reality of what Jonathan Edwards concluded to his congregation in his farewell sermon after being fired by them:

> I pray God to pity you, and take care of you, and provide for you the best means for the good of your souls, and that God himself would undertake for you to be your heavenly Father, and the mighty Redeemer of your immortal souls. Do not neglect to pray for yourselves. Take heed you be not of the number of those who cast off fear, and restrain prayer before God. Constantly pray to God in secret, and often remember that great day when you must appear before the judgment seat of Christ, and meet your minister there, who has so often counseled and warned you.[2]

Because of the eternal relationship between pastors and their people portrayed in this final chapter of Hebrews, so much more is at stake in the mass exodus of pastors from their churches than a career change. Endurance not merely affirms a true faith in Jesus, but also solidifies a pastor's faithfulness toward those entrusted to his care until the Chief Shepherd returns.

This is why the great Puritan pastor John Flavel exhorted every pastor to look to the fruit of that enduring faithfulness:

> O Brethren! Who would not study and pray, spend and be spent, in the service of such a bountiful Master! Is it not worth all our labours and sufferings, to come with all those souls we instrumentally begat to Christ: and all that we edified, established, confirmed, and comforted in the way to heaven; and say, Lord, here am I, and the children thou hast given me? To hear one spiritual child say, Lord, this is the minister by whom I believed: Another, this is he, by whom I was edified, established, and comforted. This is the man that resolved my doubts, quickened my dying affections, reduced my soul, when wandering from the truth![3]

May God, by his Spirit and grace, spur us on to endure in our divine appointments all the more with joy, regardless of the hardship and difficulties. May we remember these implications from the end of the letter to the Hebrews, and allow them to empower us to hold fast until the Chief Shepherd appears and we receive the unfading crown of glory promised to all those who faithfully shepherd his people (1 Peter 5:4).

Reflect on these points

1. *"As pastors, we of all people should recognize and be most grateful for so many who, by God's sovereign grace, were placed in our lives to lead us faithfully, speak God's Word to us, and live lives that we should*

imitate." Reflect on those who have prayed for you, taught you, and invested in you and your ministry as fuel to press on.

2. *"If our calling is to lead God's people to follow Jesus faithfully, it requires jumping to the front of the line and taking them outside the camp. When we wallow in our difficulties and discouragements because they are hard (and they really are sometimes), I don't think we realize that we are telling our people to go outside the camp (where Jesus is) while we hang back." Reflect on our calling from our Chief Shepherd to lead our people in following Christ outside the camp, and what adjustments in your life need to be made to take them there.*

3. *"Let us not forget that our calling to keep watch over the souls of our people is a great, joyful burden that is unlike anything else we experience. It will and should consume us … Until we feel the weight of that burden and embrace it, we will not experience the tremendous joy that comes from that burden." Reflect on the people you shepherd and consider the weighty reality of the eternal account you will give to the Chief Shepherd for their souls.*

Conclusion

The progression of faithful saints who demonstrated a genuine, enduring faith in Jesus did not stop once the Bible was completed. In fact, the suffering and persecution endured by the early church serves as a template for those who followed the same Master after them. Saints such as Augustine, Knox, Luther, Calvin, Bunyan, Brainerd, Judson, Carey, Paton, Elliot, and many others, all undeniably prove the cost of following Christ and the requirement for holding fast through that cost. The church throughout the last two thousand years has seen men, women, and even children "of whom the world was not worthy" (Heb. 11:38). This list continues to grow today. We are inspired to follow in their footsteps as we seek to persevere in our faith in Jesus just as they did.

We all know of Christians who are enduring their own unique hardships, sufferings, and trials that are causing them to grow weary in the race and who are tempted to give up. Nevertheless, they press on. They endure. Therefore, in conclusion, I would like to give a few examples of those in my own life who are not famous—no one would write about them in a book of martyrs—but who inspire me to fix my eyes on Jesus, to consider him, because of how tenaciously they persevered (or continue to persevere) in order to finish the race well. I want to introduce you to a pastor, a missionary, a family member, and a church member.

Pastor

I met Ferrell over ten years ago. By the time I met him he had served faithfully as a pastor for over forty years and was "retired." Retirement for him meant doing pastoral care part-time at a large church, preaching at every funeral he got called for, and preaching somewhere most Sundays. He was a simple man with very little education. Yet he had led hundreds to the Lord, preached faithfully throughout his ministry, and, because of his zealous shepherding of the sick, was nicknamed "the master of the hospital room." Probably the most striking mark of perseverance in his ministry was how he spent his final day on this earth. On an Easter Sunday, he preached at a church in the morning. He preached at another church in the evening. Then, while getting ready for bed that night, he had a massive heart attack and died. What a way for a lifelong, faithful preacher of the gospel to leave this world! He had preached the resurrection of Jesus in the morning. He had preached the resurrection in the evening. Then, before the end of the night, his soul experienced the resurrection and met the Lord Jesus! Without question, this man endured in his faith firm until the end. His widow continues to hold fast to Christ in inspiring ways.

Missionary

My dear friend John is currently a missionary serving in one of the areas in the world where Christians are most severely persecuted. He has suffered many illnesses and endured persecution of his own, but the greatest test of his faith came when his eldest daughter almost died several times while they served in a disease-infested mission field. The family returned to America to save the daughter's life through medical treatment, and most assumed that they would not go back to the mission field. Not so. In fact, they left for an even more dangerous and difficult mission field than before, and this is where John and his family currently serve. John is, for me, one of the most moving examples of one who does not "shrink back" (Heb. 10:39) but is faithfully holding fast to Christ.

Family member

My grandmother was possibly the sweetest, kindest person I have known. She served her family as if it was the greatest love of her life. She sacrificially cared for many as her lifelong friends, but none of these things brought her the hope she needed in her greatest time of need. The one hope she had was her belief in the truth of what Jesus declared about himself: "I am the resurrection and the life; he who believes in Me will live even if he dies" (John 11:25–26).

What she believed about Jesus was confirmed time and time again on the Fridays we would spend with her, when she would ask questions about the Bible study she was doing, discuss issues concerning her church with a gospel perspective in mind, or just daily demonstrate a faith in Christ and trust in his purposes.

At the age of eighty-five, she was diagnosed with terminal cancer. Her faith and trust in Christ were powerfully affirmed even more in her final two months. I sat with her the day after she received the news about the cancer and she acknowledged how hard this would be, but she then declared her trust in Christ to see her through it. I saw that trust in Christ as the pain in her back became excruciating; she cried to Jesus for comfort. I saw that trust in Jesus when I sat in the hospital with her the final day she was alert enough to have a conversation and she asked me to read God's Word to her. I would read her passages about the hope we have in Christ from sin and death. Often she would say, "Read that one again."

She believed this, and it empowered her to hold fast to Christ firm to the end (Heb. 3:14). Now she has the privilege of having experienced fully the reality behind Paul's words: "To live is Christ and to die is gain" (Phil. 1:21). She has now received and experienced the full inheritance of which only the Son is worthy yet which he purchased for us by giving his own life.

Church member

During my time at my church, there have been many folk who have died and gone to be with the Lord, but I have known few who have impacted me so deeply and personally as Marie did during the six years I served as her pastor. Her encouragement, support, care, optimism, and unshakable faith in her Savior challenged everyone who knew her.

For years she was the first person who greeted others at church because she was there before anyone else, making coffee for the Sunday-school class, though she didn't even drink coffee. One of the many ways she impacted me was by God using her to bring an encouraging word at the most needed time. During a challenging time in my church, when most letters I received were complaints, I regularly received notes like this one from Marie:

Thank you for all you are doing and your faithfulness as our pastor. I have prayed for decades that the Lord would send a faithful man of God to our church and the Lord has answered my prayers in you. Press on. Stay faithful. Our great God and Savior, Jesus Christ, is enough to give you strength through any difficulty you face.

She has always had, and will always have, a special place with me and act as a model of a faithful, enduring follower of Christ.

You have these same kinds of people in your life. As they impact you, allow their enduring faith to act as an example and inspiration to you, just as those in Hebrews 11 were intended. Most of all, allow your enduring faith to inspire others. Fix your eyes on Jesus (Heb. 12:2), so that others around you will look to him. Consider him (12:3), so that your family will take note that Christ's suffering on your behalf is what empowers you to go on when others would give up. Look to Christ, so that the testimony of your life—just like those I have described above—is undeniably and unquestionably a demonstration of a true, enduring faith in Jesus.

Endnotes

Introduction

1 This story is well captured in Alfred Lansing, *Endurance: Shackleton's Incredible Voyage* (New York: Basic Books, 1999).

2 Wayne Grudem, *Systematic Theology* (Grand Rapids, MI: Zondervan, 1994), p. 788.

3 All emphasis in Scripture quotations is the author's.

4 David Helm, *The Big Picture Story Bible* (Wheaton, IL: Crossway, 2004), p. 19.

Ch. 3 Enduring … like Isaac, Jacob, and Joseph

1 Originally written in the Abstract of Principles of 1859.

2 "The Need of Decision for the Truth," in *The Sword and the Trowel* (March 1874); available from The Spurgeon Archive, at: www.spurgeon.org/. Accessed July 2011.

3 Richard Sibbes, "Christ Is Best: or, St Paul's Strait," available at www.puritansermons. com/. Accessed July 2011.

Ch. 6 Enduring … through soaring and suffering

1 H. C. G. Moule, *Charles Simeon* (London: Intervarsity, 1948), pp. 155–156.

Ch. 8 A final word to pastors

1 Quoted in Mark E. Dever, *A Display of God's Glory: Basics of Church Structure* (Washington DC: 9Marks), p. 42.

2 Jonathan Edwards, "A Farewell Sermon," July 1, 1750; available at http://truthinheart. com/EarlyOberlinCD/CD/Edwards/Sermons/Farewell.htm. Accessed July 2011.

3 John Flavel, "The Character of a Complete Evangelical Pastor Drawn by Christ," in *The Works of John Flavel*, vol. 6 (Carlisle: Banner of Truth, 1997), p. 579.

About Day One:

Day One's threefold commitment:

- To be faithful to the Bible, God's inerrant, infallible Word;
- To be relevant to our modern generation;
- To be excellent in our publication standards.

I continue to be thankful for the publications of Day One. They are biblical; they have sound theology; and they are relevant to the issues at hand. The material is condensed and manageable while, at the same time, being complete—a challenging balance to find. We are happy in our ministry to make use of these excellent publications.

JOHN MACARTHUR, PASTOR-TEACHER, GRACE COMMUNITY CHURCH, CALIFORNIA

It is a great encouragement to see Day One making such excellent progress. Their publications are always biblical, accessible and attractively produced, with no compromise on quality. Long may their progress continue and increase!

JOHN BLANCHARD, AUTHOR, EVANGELIST AND APOLOGIST

Visit our web site for more information and
to request a free catalogue of our books.
www.dayone.co.uk

U.S. web site:
www.dayonebookstore.com

A faith that endures
Also available

In the care of the Good Shepherd
Meditations on Psalm 23

IAIN D CAMPBELL

112PP, PAPERBACK

ISBN 978-1-84625-175-7

There is probably no passage of Scripture with which people are more familiar than the twenty-third psalm. The words of the metrical version are among the best loved and most often sung of our Scottish Metrical Psalms. Every statement of the psalm is loaded with meaning and with significance and importance. Enjoy reading through these inspiring meditations on Psalm 23.

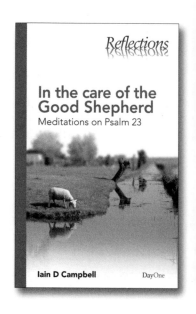

'Iain D. Campbell's exposition of Psalm 23 is masterful, both exegetically and pastorally. Reminiscent of the late Douglas MacMillan's work on this psalm, Dr Campbell's adds significantly to our appreciation of the psalm; indeed, under his guidance we are led to behold new vistas of greener pastures and still waters. Sure-footed expository genius of a rare kind.'
DEREK THOMAS, REFORMED THEOLOGICAL SEMINARY, JACKSON, MISSISSIPPI, USA

'The book is written by one who functions as an under-shepherd of the Saviour and who is aware of the spiritual needs and desires of his flock, and this experience is very much to the fore throughout the work. Further, the activities of Jesus are described in such a straightforward devotional manner that makes the book a joy to read. It is a book suitable for the heart as well as for the mind.'
REVD DR MALCOLM MACLEAN, MINISTER, SCALPAY FREE CHURCH OF SCOTLAND